RABBI JESUS

Learning from the Master Teacher

Rabbi Jesus
Learning from the Master Teacher

Stephen D. Jones

PEAKE ROAD

Macon, Georgia

ISBN 1-57312-099-5

Rabbi Jesus
Learning from the Master Teacher

Stephen D. Jones

Copyright © 1997

Peake Road
6316 Peake Road
Macon, Georgia 31210-3960
1-800-747-3016

All rights reserved.
Printed in the United States of America.

Biblical quotations, unless otherwise noted, are from the
New Revised Standard Version of the Bible (NRSV).

The paper used in this publication
meets the minimum requirements of
American National Standard for Information Sciences—
Permanence of Paper for Printed Library Materials.
ANSI Z39.48–1984

Library of Congress Cataloging-in-Publication

Jones, Stephen D.
    Rabbi Jesus: learning from the master teacher/
        Stephen D. Jones.
        viii + 88 pp.   6" x 9" (15 x 23 cm.)
        Includes bibliographical references.
        ISBN 1-57312-099-5   (alk. paper)
        1. Jesus Christ—Teaching methods. I. Title.
    BT590.T5J64   1997
    232.9'04—dc21   96-37170
                                                                   CIP

"For too long the world has
heard the church, rather than the church's teacher."

"Rabbi Jesus belongs on both sides of the crucifixion."

Contents

Introduction
Call Me Teacher and Lord   1

Chapter 1
Jesus as First-Century Rabbi   11

Chapter 2
Jesus as Charismatic Teacher   31

Chapter 3
Jesus as Subversive Sage   37

Chapter 4
Jesus as Transforming Teacher   47

Chapter 5
Jesus as Lover of Questions   57

Chapter 6
Jesus as Risen Rabbi   63

Chapter 7
The Teacher Is Here and Is Calling for You   71

Chapter 8
They Had Been with Jesus   77

Song
You Say a Teacher He Can Be   87

Introduction
Call Me Teacher and Lord

Although the church knows Jesus as a great teacher who told parables and taught the Beatitudes, it has never been completely comfortable with a focus upon Jesus as rabbi. As condemning as the admission sounds, such a focus seems "too Jewish" to a largely gentile church, given the claims of Jesus as Lord and Savior. We assume that Jews would assign Jesus the role of "just another rabbi." To Christians, Jesus is God's "only begotten Son."

Christians have been reluctant to align ourselves anywhere near those who would say, "Jesus is only a human teacher." In this perspective, Jesus as teacher seems to refute Jesus the Christ, the incarnation of God. Many believe that Jesus as teacher describes him before the crucifixion, and Jesus as Lord and Savior describes him after the resurrection. Jesus as teacher signifies something less than his divinely intended role. Little wonder the church has tended to avoid the idea of Jesus as rabbi.

Yet many scholars today argue that we will not understand Jesus until we see him as a first-century Jew. This is not because admitting his Jewishness is suddenly politically correct, but because Jesus was a Jewish rabbi in a thoroughly Jewish context. If we overlook this fact, we miss his message. How much Jesus stepped beyond his Jewish audience and tradition is open for debate; that he intended his message for his fellow Jews is not.

The church today, so diverse in all of its expressions, likely converges around the theological confession of Jesus as Lord and Savior. This confession may mean something different depending upon the believer with whom you are speaking, but it means something to most believers. Yet there are only three occurrences of the title Savior, referring to Jesus, in the four Gospels (Luke 1:69, 2:11; John 4:42). Yet they speak frequently of Jesus as Lord and rabbi. Jesus is addressed as Lord no fewer than 83 times, and as rabbi or teacher 56 times. (The next most frequently used title for Jesus is the enigmatic Son of man, found no fewer than 37 times.)

On the other hand, the letters of the early church contained in the New Testament have almost no reference to Jesus as rabbi or teacher. Written much closer to his lifetime, they reflect how the earliest followers were awestruck and captivated by Jesus as crucified and resurrected Lord. There may be brief acknowledgments of Jesus Christ as a teacher (for example, 1 John 2:27; 2 John 9-10; Eph 4:20-24), but there is an inferred recognition that this role has been superseded by Jesus as Lord and Savior. Jesus as teacher is never compellingly articulated in the early church's original correspondence. Through the centuries, the church has more consistently repeated the language of the Letters than of the Gospels.

Because of the church's reluctance to claim Jesus as rabbi, the theological work of asking what relevance Rabbi Jesus has to the church of resurrection faith largely remains to be done. Rabbi Jesus belongs on both sides of the crucifixion. For his disciples, Jesus is the Teacher through his life, death, and resurrection. Are not his death and resurrection the most provocative areas of learning for any Christian? Why else do we celebrate Lent but to enter into the richness of this learning, over and over again? The concept of Jesus as teacher need not diminish but rather fulfill what God sent Jesus to be.

To Christians, Jesus is the best representation we have of God. Jesus is not all there is of God, but as the Second Person of the Trinity is the most tangible expression of God. Therefore, Jesus is the one who teaches us who God is, not just by what he teaches, but by revealing himself as teacher.

This book seeks to reconnect the church today with the Gospel way of identifying and relating to Jesus as rabbi or teacher. One reason for increased awareness is that most modern translations no longer translate the Greek word *didaskalos* as "master," but rather, more accurately, as "teacher." This occurs in forty-nine instances in the Gospels where today we are reading teacher, or, in one case, instructor. In the King James Version, the word rabbi was often translated as master (eight instances), whereas in most modern translations the title rabbi is actually used. To illustrate, following are examples of the New Revised Standard Version (listed first) of *didaskalos* compared to the traditional King James Version.

Teacher, I will follow you wherever you go.
Master, I will follow thee whithersoever thou goest.
(Matt 8:19b)

Why does your teacher eat with tax collectors and sinners?
Why eateth your master with publicans and sinners?
(Matt 9:11b)

Teacher, I brought you my son.
Master, I have brought unto thee my son.
(Mark 9:17b)

Teacher, what must I do to inherit eternal life?
Master, what shall I do to inherit eternal life?
(Luke 10:25b)

You call me Teacher and Lord.
Ye call me Master and Lord.
(John 13:13a)

In the King James Version, the term master is used in the Gospels sixty-two times; in the New Revised Standard Version, typical of the newer translations, its use is reduced. In this new translation, there are only six occasions—all in Luke—when Master is used as a title for Jesus, translating the word *epistata,* meaning "manager" or "superintendent."[1]

Not only has Jesus as rabbi begun to emerge in the newer English translations of the Bible, but Jesus in his role as rabbi has begun to emerge from the writings of biblical scholars as they share their increasingly impressive discoveries of first-century Jewish life. In chapter 1, I highlight some of these discoveries, offering a more pronounced understanding of Jesus as a first-century rabbi.

What's the Difference?

Does it really matter what we call Jesus? What's in a name, anyway, whether it be Savior, or Lord, or Rabbi? Does it not matter more who he is to us than what we call him? Is it not just semantics?

I can speak from my own experience. Calling Jesus "Teacher" and "Rabbi" has stirred a spiritual awakening within me. It has made an opening in my assumptions about Jesus and in my relationship with him. My prayer life has been transformed by listening to and for the Rabbi. As a disciple, I find that relating to Jesus as living rabbi has enlivened and disciplined my faith-walk.

When I walked into Mrs. Conlon's public school class in the fifth grade, I hadn't much of an idea about teachers, other than their power over my life. But Mrs. Conlon was a teacher! And it didn't take long to recognize that. She worked me harder at a time in my life when I wanted to work less and, in so doing, stirred something within me. If, in the fifth grade, someone had introduced me to Jesus as teacher, I believe it would have been a profound discovery because of my respect and esteem for Mrs. Conlon. Another teacher, beginning in the ninth grade, was Mr. Ward. In him I saw the authentic humanity of a teacher. In seminary Chuck Melchert taught me respect for great ideas. Then there was Mrs. Weaver, a teacher with almost no education or formal training, who loved the hell out of the little hellions in her third grade Sunday School class. She taught me the power of teacher as agent of transformation.

Each of these persons have made the term teacher bigger than it would ever have been without them. They were real teachers, true teachers. My life is profoundly different because they were my teachers. They became the standard by which I have evaluated others who have carried the title but did not have the authoritative relationship.

Jesus as rabbi or teacher awakens something out of my "Mrs. Weaver-Mrs. Conlon-Mr. Ward-Chuck Melchert" tradition. He is all of that, and more. Surely without them, I might not know what a teacher could be. Would not all of our lives be much less without encountering those teachers who expected and recognized our highest and best?

I think a great deal is in a name—my name, yours, and the name or title we give Jesus. My efforts here are not to lead people away from the confession of Jesus as Lord and Savior. That statement of faith means much to me. I only intend to augment and evoke new ideas and avenues, and perhaps even a more profound relationship with the one whom we call Jesus Christ. As Eduard Schweizer said,

The church must continue to make fresh statements of who Jesus is. It can never reduce these statements to a single final formula that would define Jesus for the rest of time. If it did so, it would be lord over Jesus, and he would no longer be Lord of the church.[2]

Portraits of Jesus

Events are laden. They are heavy with a thousand causes. They are luminous with a thousand references. They laugh or cry with a thousand feelings.

—Bernard Lee
The Galilean Jewishness of Jesus

There is no such thing as uninterpreted history. History is interpretation. Interpretation implies a worldview, a conceptual framework, a philosophical stance on the part of the interpreter, whether acknowledged or not.

—Frederick J. Murphy
The Religious World of Jesus

We must have some kind of position, some kind of vantage-point or perspective, if we are to see and understand anything. A work of art, for example, . . . cannot be seen at all except from a vantagepoint. It can be viewed from this or that angle, but it cannot be observed from no angle at all. The same is true of history. We cannot obtain a view of the past except from the place where we are standing at the moment. . . . To imagine that one can have historical objectivity without a perspective is an illusion.

—Albert Nolan
Jesus Before Christianity

It would be possible to tell a story about Martin Luther King, Jr. as a man who did not grow up in poverty, was too moderate for many African-American leaders in the civil rights struggle, was suspected of plagiarism in his doctoral research, and needlessly incited events that caused a lot of cities to burn. If I were to hear such an interpretation of King's life, I would be enraged. That is not the picture of King in my memory, however. There may be partial truth to these so-called facts, but I want to know why a person would focus upon those things when so many others are available that tell a much different story.

In the three months my family spent in South Africa in 1992, the history of that nation, or its future, was described in dramatically different ways, depending upon which racial group was speaking. The heritage of apartheid was still very much a factor in the way different racial groups viewed their society. The white Afrikaners tended to have a very definite understanding. The English people had a different understanding. The so-called "coloureds" had yet another, as did the Indian people and the black Africans.

All history is interpretation. If you were too young to experience the 1960s, the only way you can know about that decade is from eyewitnesses, whether from personal conversation or their writing. And who you ask will determine the perspective offered. "Just give me the facts," we might plead. But my definition of the facts, or the facts I choose to give you, color the perspective.

History is meaning-making, not fact-dispensing. Ask someone who is a devoted follower of a famous teacher, and you get a certain picture of the person. Ask another who is a skeptic or enemy, and you get an entirely different picture.

All history is interpretation. We don't have a color photograph of Jesus in the Gospels; we have "a set of portraits," according to Jaroslav Pelikar's description in *Jesus Through the Centuries*. We look at him through the colors on the brush that each artist chooses to use, the pose each gives of him, the interpretation.

We need "artists" to paint portraits of Jesus, both then and now— portraits of how he lived and taught then, portraits of how he lives and can teach now. Thanks be to God for the varied richness of the four portraits of Jesus in the four Gospels. Yet as a follower of a living rabbi, I cannot be content to leave him back in the first century. I must try to find those connections that help me experience the presence of the Rabbi today in as real and sure terms as he was present then.

In chapters 2–6, I offer five portraits of Jesus as rabbi and teacher, all of which originate in the Gospels. Some may appeal more to you than others. Some may bring Jesus more to life for you, the way some paintings seem to come alive before our eyes. I offer the five sketches because we must first be able to envision Jesus as rabbi and teacher. My goal is to stir the rich artistry and visionary spirit within you. Once a portrait of Rabbi Jesus speaks to you, I pray you will allow Jesus to have an active, teaching role in your life.

Some might question why it is important to depend upon one's imagination in approaching Jesus as rabbi, but just as all of art and literature depend upon the imagination, so does prayer. Prayer is envisioning within the one we cannot see. Without vision, faith falters. We cannot follow behind Rabbi Jesus on the dusty Palestinian roads. We cannot literally sit at his feet. We cannot hear his audible voice. Yet we can use our gifts and imagination to envision a spiritual encounter.

What's Missing

I am trained as an educator in the church. I am deeply concerned about the teaching and learning that occur within the local church. If you go into a typical Protestant church, you will likely find more volunteers committed to teaching than to any other ministry. You will find the board of Christian education, by whatever name it is called, to be one of the busiest and most dedicated groups there. And, in most churches, outside of worship, more people connect with the church through a class or small group that presumably has been organized for teaching, learning, and spiritual growth than any other structure.

Yet, teaching and learning in the church today seem to lack a true mandate. We do it because it was done to us. We do it because it is the best avenue for authentic connection with friends in the congregation. We do it for fellowship. We might even do it for informational study about the Bible.

Two things seem to be missing as the church confronts the ministry of teaching and learning today, whether it is a mainline church, a Pentecostal church, an ethnic church, a Roman Catholic Church, or an evangelical church.

First, Christian education is often little more than babysitting for children and fellowship groupings for adults. There is no real sense that authentic teaching and learning occur because of an educational and biblical mandate to do so. We have lost so much of the communal understanding of why teaching and learning should play a crucial role in the church today. Educators in the church lack a focus on the reasons for their ministry. We are repeating forms from the past or mimicking new ones if numerically successful elsewhere. A living rabbi will make of Christian education something unique from other worthy educational approaches. The Living Rabbi is a unique authoritative source for learning in the church. What we lack today is a calling to and from the Teacher, to be his disciples or learners.

Second, a biblical paradigm is missing from the church's teaching and learning. A biblical paradigm is needed so that we do not slavishly mimic first-century rabbinical teaching styles. That would be inappropriate for a number of reasons, not the least that Jesus is no longer present in bodily form. We cannot literally follow him down the road of our lives nor sit at his feet, but we can use the structure of Jesus as teacher in its rich and evocative biblical context. Although the Gospels suggest ways the earliest followers continued interaction with Jesus as their risen rabbi, this paradigm needs to be utterly contemporary. There is no such thing as good generic teaching. There is only teaching that speaks directly and profoundly to and with the learner. We are the disciples today, not Peter and John, not Mary and Martha. A biblical paradigm of teaching will bring the Rabbi and the Rabbi's wisdom alive and make it authoritative in our midst. The church is most authentic when it employs symbols and paradigms from its biblical heritage. We have within the Bible itself a profound model for teaching and learning between the Rabbi and his disciples.

Conclusion

If we are to authentically confront Jesus the Living Teacher, there is theological work to be done. We must make Jesus accessible to each generation (evangelical work), discover the Second Person of the Trinity as the incarnational teacher (christological work), see Jesus authentically portrayed as a teacher in the Gospels (biblical work), and cultivate connections to the Living Teacher (spiritual work). Perhaps the spiritual work will prove the most fruitful and the least explored. In the final chapter I examine this theological work and also offer seven spiritual disciplines that can help Jesus' followers meet him as a living rabbi.

To the extent that we have seen a distinction between spiritual growth and Christian education, a meeting with Rabbi Jesus tends to diminish that. Christian education not only focuses upon what the Teacher taught 2,000 years ago, but even more helps us meet the Living Teacher today and become transformed through that meeting. No other expression of education has this as its focus. Christian education has as its goal introducing people to the Teacher, not just offering historical information about him. This goal explains my view of Jesus as rabbi and teacher through his risky and liberating interactions with women. I have been amazed at how powerfully these interactions translate into the kind of teaching and learning we need in the church. Each of the portraits in this book arise from his relationship in scripture with women.

May we who are passionately involved in the church's teaching and learning realize that something is profoundly missing. May we learn, in all its richness, to approach Jesus as he asked us: "Call me Teacher and Lord . . . for that is what I am."

Notes

[1] The term master, used in my childhood in a Southern border state, was a too-clear reference to a master-slave relationship. It evoked no image of a teacher. This was enhanced by the other use in the Gospels, "master of the house," which still appears in the New Revised Standard Version.

[2] Eduard Schweizer, *Jesus* (Atlanta: John Knox Press, 1971) 189.

Chapter 1
Jesus as First-Century Rabbi
Luke 10:39

>"Fairest Lord Jesus"
>"O, How I Love Jesus"
>"Jesus Is Tenderly Calling"
>"Tell Me the Story of Jesus"
>"Jesus Is All the World to Me"
>"Tis So Sweet to Trust in Jesus"
>"What a Friend We Have in Jesus"
>"Since Jesus Came into My Heart"

Nearly all the hymns I sang in church growing up in the Ozark Mountains were about Jesus. As a child, I never thought much about God. It was as if we were unitarians, except that Jesus was the only "person" of God we talked about. We prayed to Jesus and sang to Jesus. Jesus was in my heart. Everywhere I went, he went with me. He wanted to be my closest friend.

Later, during my rebellious young adult years, I put Jesus back in the first century and introduced myself to God as creator, and drew myself into the mystery and transcendence of God, the part of God that was beyond me. I remained unitarian in emphasis; I just traded in Jesus for God.

With Jesus no longer in my heart, but back in the first century, the question eventually became, "What do I do with Jesus?" So much of my adult search has been an attempt to answer that question. One day I realized there were deep and secret chambers of my heart from which Jesus had never really departed. And while Jesus was a person of the first century, he also belongs in this century. And one way for him to be in this century is if I make place for him in my heart, in my experience, in my trusting places, in my prayers, in my embodied faith, in my expectations, in my risk taking.

I began to develop a Christology, an understanding of who Jesus is, not only for me, but for the world today. But in order to know what to do with Jesus today, it became necessary to see him back then, for who he was.

Throughout this century, scholars have been trying to answer the question, "Who was Jesus in the first century?" As a result, we may know more about Jesus as a person of his own day than any time since the second century. Howard Clark Kee and Marcus Borg affirm this.

> In spite of (the) range of ways in which the tradition about Jesus has been transmitted, we have available a clear and remarkably consistent array of evidence about this figure whose life, teachings, and death have continued to have such a profound and enduring impact on the subsequent history of the human race.[1]

> We can in fact know as much about Jesus as we can any figure in the ancient world. . . . We can sketch a fairly full and historically defensible portrait of Jesus.[2]

Of course, there were eyewitnesses in the first century who knew Jesus and faithfully cherished the stories about him and told them in an amazing oral tradition. We are descendants in faith of those original eyewitnesses. Scholars today have been unpacking their stories and oral tradition. They have made revealing discoveries from archaeology, from more recently-discovered ancient gospels and manuscripts, and by comparing alternative first-century sources. In addition, they are overcoming centuries of anti-Semitism to see Jesus as a first-century Palestinian Jew. Frederick Murphy explains the change in perspective this way:

> Even when Christians try to take the humanity of Jesus fully into account, there has traditionally been a reluctance to make him too much of a Jew. Rather, it is his uniqueness that has been emphasized. How he differed from his fellow Jews has been stressed, not how he was the same. The result is that the Jewishness of Jesus has faded. He becomes a universal, a person without a homeland, native language, traditional religion. The trend begins as early as the New Testament. For example, Jesus is often portrayed as speaking with "the Jews." That is indeed a strange way to talk, given that Jesus is a Jew. This way of talking sets Jesus apart from the Jews, almost denying that he is one of them. To ask how Jesus related to the Jews of his day makes about as much sense as asking how a modern American college student relates to "Americans."[3]

As with any person of history, we have only interpretations of Jesus' life by those who remembered him in a certain way for their own purposes. But with increasing and surprising confidence, a picture of Jesus as a first-century Jew is coming more clearly into focus.

Reintroducing Jesus as Rabbi

What did Jesus' disciples in the first century call him? How did they view him? How did Jesus enter the trusting places of their hearts? We can say with ever-increasing confidence that those first disciples knew him as Rabbi Jesus. Rabbi was their word for teacher. According to Bernard J. Lee,

> That Jesus was a teacher, that just about everyone around Jesus related to him as a teacher, and that Jesus thought of himself as a teacher: the Gospels are uniformly and strongly of one voice on this piece of history.[4]

The verb teach was frequently used to describe Jesus' activity. He taught in the cities, villages, and streets (Luke 13:22, 26). He taught along the Sea of Galilee (Mark 2:13) and from a boat just off the shore (Luke 5:3). He taught regularly in the synagogues of Galilee (Luke 4:15); in the synagogue of Nazareth where he was raised (Mark 6:2); and in the synagogue of Capernaum, his adult home (Luke 4:31). He also taught in the south, across the Jordan from Judea (Mark 10:1-2) and most notably in the temple at Jerusalem (Luke 19:47; John 7:14, 8:20). When Jesus was questioned at his trial about his teaching, he reminded Caiaphas, the high priest, that he had always taught very openly in the synagogues and temple.[5]

Since the Gospels were written nearly a generation after Jesus' crucifixion, as persons of the early church remembered the sayings of Jesus, they naturally inserted the titles used for Jesus in their daily worship and praise, most frequently the title Lord. In the Gospel of Matthew, there are twenty-one references to Jesus as Lord. Yet the disciples may have rarely if ever called Jesus "Lord" during his lifetime. They were slow to recognize Jesus' fullest identity. Also the Jews as a people were careful to keep holy the names for God. If indeed they called Jesus "Lord," it certainly would have been as a respectful title for a teacher, not with the fuller meaning of the resurrected Lord, an event that had not yet taken place. In Greek, the word *kyrie* translates as master, sir, or lord. Therefore, according to H. L. Ellison, "we are probably safe in assuming that where Jesus is called Lord, it normally represents Rabbi."[6]

Jaroslav Pelikan believes we are justified in concluding that

> the title "teacher" or "master" (*didaskalos* in the Greek New Testament) was intended as a translation of that name [rabbi], [and] it seems safe to say that it was as a rabbi that Jesus was known and addressed by his immediate followers and by others.[7]

If the ancient Greek manuscripts are recalling the word rabbi, whether translated as "teacher," "rabbi," or the respectful "rabbouni," I suspect we need both titles today. We need the title rabbi because of the reminder that Jesus was a Jew and his teachings occurred in a first-century Jewish context of gathering disciples, not just casual students. Yet we need the title teacher in order to be clear about the role Jesus played and continues to play.

Jesus was not called teacher or rabbi in any of Paul's letters, the earliest writings in the New Testament. We can therefore conclude that the Gospel writers had no compelling reason to call Jesus "Rabbi" unless it was a title used of him frequently during his ministry years and entered the Gospels through the oral tradition that faithfully retained the stories of Jesus' life. It was a most authentic Jewish title. Bernard Lee listed the following characters in the Gospels as calling Jesus "Teacher":

- people in general (Matt 17:24), for example, a voice from the crowd (Matt 19:16), Jesus' own disciples (Mark 4:38, 13:1), and sometimes the disciples by name (Mark 10:35; Luke 5:5, 7:40)
- important people, such as the rich young man (Mark 10:17), the family of the head of the synagogue (Mark 5:35), the Pharisees (Mark 4:14; Matt 19:11), the Sadducees (Mark 12:19, 8:19), and the spies of the chief priests and scribes (Luke 20:21)
- the culturally despicable, for instance, lepers (Luke 17:13) and tax collectors (Luke 3:12)
- Jesus himself: "The Teacher asks, Where is my guest room where I may eat the Passover with my disciples?" (Mark 14:14).[8]

After Lord, teacher or rabbi is the next most frequent title appearing in the Gospels. In Luke there are 13 references, 15 in John, and 12 in Matthew. In Mark, the earliest Gospel, teacher or rabbi is the most frequently used title for Jesus, occurring 16 times. In addition, there are 18 other references in Mark, specifically mentioning the activity of teaching in describing Jesus' ministry. Jesus' teaching incidents literally fill the Gospel pages.

Yet how many times have we heard Jesus referred to as rabbi? How many prayers have we addressed to "Jesus, our teacher"? How many of our prayers have concluded, "In the name of Rabbi Jesus, amen"? How many of our hymns refer to Jesus as rabbi or teacher?

Over the centuries, Rabbi Jesus has nearly drifted from our view, out of distance of our hearing. We may focus upon his teachings in Bible study, but we do not think of Jesus as *our* teacher. He may have been a pre-crucifixion teacher, but not a post-resurrection teacher. Yet, if we go back to the four Gospels, we find that we have selectively overlooked what is there.

Why? What happened? For one who was so clearly known as rabbi or teacher, why is this language absent from the church's earliest correspondence? And why has it been so absent from the church's confessions and doctrines down through the centuries? And why so absent from the church's prayers and meditative heritage? Even when the church speaks of its educational ministries, it is unusual for it to do so in the name of Rabbi Jesus. Jaroslav Pelikan reasoned,

> To the Christian disciples of the first century the conception of Jesus as a rabbi was self-evident, to the Christian disciples of the second century it was embarrassing, to the Christian disciples of the third century and beyond it was obscure.[9]

The earliest disciples were obviously not ready for all the new realities of Jesus' sudden death and resurrection. They knew Jesus as their rabbi, their teacher. They knew what that meant, because it conformed to a familiar pattern in their society. Jesus may have been an unorthodox rabbi in some ways, but he was a rabbi nonetheless. The disciples knew what it felt like to sit at the feet of the Rabbi and learn or to follow a respectful distance behind him. Of this Eduard Schweizer wrote,

> The death of Jesus at first made an end of the disciples following him. Discipleship can no longer have the form of a real walking behind him. Thus the church has never quite overcome her hesitation about extending the expression, "following Jesus" to the time after his death.[10]

But what happened when your rabbi died? Traditionally, you revered him. You honored him by committing his teachings to memory. Perhaps you continued the rabbinical school left behind in his memory. But none of this matches the experiences of the earliest disciples. Far from committing the writings and teachings of Rabbi Jesus to memory, these disciples were experiencing an explosive, transforming encounter with a resurrected Christ. No longer could they sit at the feet of this rabbi or follow him down the road. Every way in which they had known Jesus as rabbi no longer fit their new experiences. And so they let go of that language and came to speak of Jesus as Lord and Savior. And today it is as if this first language never existed, even though it is there, remembered by the eyewitnesses to his life, in the writings of the four Gospels.

First-Century Rabbis

The first century was a revolutionary time for Judaism. After the destruction of Jerusalem in C.E. 70, Pharisaic Judaism ascended to reshape Judaic faith and give an identifiable and certain meaning to the term rabbi. Those who held the title began to meet stricter qualifications and standards for ordination.

Prior to this date, and during Jesus' life, rabbis were a familiar part of the Jewish landscape, but their role was much more fluid. In Matthew 23:2, 7b, Jesus says, "The scribes and the Pharisees sit on Moses' seat. . . . [They love] to have people call them rabbi." We certainly know that Jesus did not invent the category of Jewish rabbi. Indeed, in many ways he fit the expected role. We see this in the way strangers, and even his detractors, came up to him and comfortably addressed him as rabbi.

The categories of teachers and disciples were likely borrowed by the Pharisees from the Greeks. To the Greeks, a person was called a disciple when he bound himself to someone in order to acquire his practical and theoretical knowledge.

He may be an apprentice in a trade, a student of medicine, or a member of a philosophical school. One can only be a (disciple) in the company of a *didaskalos,* a master or teacher, to whom the (disciples) since the days of the Sophists generally had to pay a fee.[11]

In New Testament Greek, two words have been translated into English as disciple. The first is *akoloutheo,* which means "to follow." Only the verb form is found in the New Testament, expressing an action. The root meaning in Greek is *path,* which literally means "to accompany or follow behind someone." The second word in Greek for disciple is *mathetes,* which appears more frequently as a noun, meaning "learner," "pupil," or "disciple."

Historically, the Jews were very reluctant to call any human being a teacher because of their conviction that God alone was their teacher. According to Vernon Robbins in *Jesus the Teacher,*

Israelite tradition prior to the Hellenistic period did not possess a fully developed social pattern of a teacher and his disciple-companions. . . . The major reason for the lack of a fully developed pattern in Israelite tradition appears to be the role of Yahweh as a summoner and teacher. Yahweh calls, commissions, and teaches wisdom and virtue in Israelite tradition. Any human teacher is simply an intermediary.[12]

Therefore, rabbi is not an expression found in the Old Testament. Even in the first century, continued Robbins, a "significant measure of reserve is exercised in the portrayal of Jewish teachers. God's function as the one who summons, teaches, and commissions remains intact."[13] However, in part because of increasing Hellenistic influence, the role of Jewish rabbis gradually became recognizable. They established a certain type of relationship with their disciples, developed their own teaching style, and were indirectly involved in making legal decisions. Likewise, Jesus took on these roles.

Rabbi/Disciple Relationship

Jesus organized his disciples into a community, much like those of other rabbis. They shared a lifestyle together, traveled together, and lived in community. Bernard Lee described the activities of first-century Jewish rabbis thus:

> The great teacher has his disciples. They travel together. They have a common fund. They prepare meals together. When they gather for a lesson in the town square or under a fig tree, others who are not disciples also gather and listen. When they travel, they are housed in local communities. The followers are sometimes older men, and sometimes married men. . . . It is immediately clear to any Christian reader how much the above description resembles the pattern and activities of Jesus and his disciples.[14]

While apparently there were not yet specific credentials required to be called a rabbi, there were expectations of having studied under another rabbi. "Jesus went up into the temple and began to teach. The Jews were astonished at it, saying, 'How does this man have such learning, when he has never been taught?'" (John 7:14-15). Jesus himself respected the role of a rabbi and used the common model of rabbi and disciple in an example: "A disciple is not above the teacher, but everyone who is fully qualified will be like the teacher" (Luke 6:40).

Jesus held in common with other rabbis an expectation for his disciples. J. Duncan Derrett explained the role like this:

> Their concept of student differed utterly from today's. It is not surprising that we distinguish "student" and "disciple," though they were once one and the same. . . . The student is a secondary son for his teacher. . . . Females might listen to a teacher's lecture, but female students as such were unknown. It was unseemly for women, unless really old, to roam about. A student must be prepared to accompany his teacher anywhere.[15]

Disciples had what we might call an "apprenticeship" to a rabbi, according to Bernard Lee.

> Martin Buber once said that a good teacher is not someone who teaches a subject well, but one who, in the course of teaching any subject, allows the student to know the world the way he or she experiences it. Good teachers guide students in their experience of reality. That kind of education presumes a prolonged and intimate contact between teacher and student.[16]

Rabbi and disciple in the first century had such a prolonged and intimate relationship, and it served as the matrix for teaching and learning. Early writings described this relationship and the resulting activities.

Learning by itself did not make a pupil, and he did not grasp the full significance of his teacher's learning in all its nuances except through prolonged intimacy with his teacher, through close association with his rich and profound mind. The disciples accompanied their sage as he went to teach, when he sat in law court, when he was engaged in the performance of meritorious deeds such as helping the poor, redeeming slaves, collecting dowries for poor brides, burying the dead, etc. The pupil took his turn preparing the common meal and catering to the general needs of the group. He performed personal services for his teacher, observed his conduct and was his respectful, loving humble companion *(T. Negaim 8:2; T.B. Pasahim 36a.)* Some laws could not be studied theoretically or merely discussed, but could only be learned by serving the teacher. The groups which consisted of a sage and his disciples had property in common, or a common fund from which food was bought. *(T.b. Erubin 73a).* Study was not confined to the school or the synagogue, but was also carried on in the vineyard, in the shade of a dove-cote, in fields, on paths under fig-trees and olives and in the market. It was not uncommon for a sage to conduct discourses and discussions with his pupils in the town-square or in the market place, with the townspeople gathering around them and listening, irrespective of whether they were able to understand all or only part of the discussion *(T. Berakoth 4:16; P.T. Berakoth II, 5c).* [17]

Teaching Style

Reciting Scripture. Jesus taught like a Jewish rabbi, often using the Jewish Scriptures in his explanations. Once the Sadducee party came up to Jesus and asked him a trick question about the resurrection of the dead, a concept they did not accept. "Teacher, Moses wrote for us that if a man's brother dies, leaving a wife but no child, the man shall marry the widow and raise up children for his brother." They continued to describe a situation in which the woman was passed from brother to brother, seven times. And then the Sadducees asked, "In the resurrection, whose wife will she be?" Like a good rabbi, Jesus quoted from the book of Moses to substantiate his position (Mark 12:18-23).

Questions. Jesus also made clever use of questions. In the Gospel of Luke, there are no fewer than 89 teaching questions; and in the Gospel of Matthew, Jesus posed 85 teaching questions! Jesus often asked rhetorical questions, "How can Satan cast out Satan?" (Mark 3:23). "Is a lamp brought in to be put under a bushel basket, or under the bed, and not on the lampstand?" (Mark 4:21). Often Jesus answered a question with a question. When confronted with the question of obedience to Caesar, he requested a coin and then asked, "Whose head is this, and whose title?" (Matt 22:20). On occasion, Jesus would answer a question with a question and refuse to give his answer until his questioners gave theirs (Matt 21:23-27).

He used questions to confront people. Turning to the assembled Pharisees, Jesus asked them, "What do you think about the Messiah? Whose son is he?" The story concludes, "No one was able to give him an answer, nor from that day did anyone dare to ask him any more questions" (Matt 22:41, 42a, 46). Rabbis were very clever in their use of questions.

Stories and Parables. Jesus often told stories and parables. "With what can we compare the kingdom of God, or what parable will we use for it?" (Mark 4:30). He chose to let his parables speak for themselves and often became annoyed when he had to explain them. "Do you not understand this parable? Then how will you understand all the parables?" (Mark 4:13). The parables were drawn from everyday experiences of Palestinian Jews of the first century.

Argumentation. Rabbis taught and interacted with one another by argumentation. For this reason, our modern depiction of the other teachers, scribes, and Jewish leaders tends to unnecessarily be that of an enemy, when it really reflects the rabbinical style of probing for the truth. The rabbis were always pressing for the truth, for wisdom, and in doing so demanded the best from the wisest. We read, "Then the Pharisees went and plotted to entrap him in what he said" (Matt 22:15). The question is whether we see this as friendly competitiveness or malice. It is depicted in verse 18, for reasons serving the purposes of the author of this Gospel, as malice. But from what we know of first-century rabbis, it could as likely have been their probing, confrontational style of wisdom seeking. Later in the same chapter (vv. 41-46), Jesus posed a question of the Pharisees, and tradition has not read malice into Jesus' intention.

Legal Interpretations

Jesus was sometimes asked to make legal decisions like a rabbi, for instance, "Teacher, tell my brother to divide the family inheritance with me" (Luke 12:13f.). His disciples sought his wisdom, as in the case of the man blind from birth. His disciples asked him, "Rabbi, who sinned, this man or his parents, that he was born blind?" (John 9:1-2). Jesus was frequently addressed as rabbi by those who were not his disciples. Nicodemus, a member of the powerful Jewish Sanhedrin, came to Jesus at night saying, "Rabbi, we know that you are a teacher who has come from God" (John 3:2).

The Rabbinical Climate

By looking at one text, we learn a great deal about Rabbi Jesus in the context of the first-century rabbinical climate. "A woman named Martha welcomed him into her home. She had a sister named Mary, who sat at the Lord's feet and listened to what he was saying" (Luke 10:38-39). This tells us Jesus was a first-century itinerant rabbi. One of the old Jewish sayings long predating Jesus was, "Let your house be a meetinghouse for the sages. Sit amidst the dust of their feet" (Aboth 1:4). We see this reenacted in Martha's home.

If extended hospitality, Jesus entered a home, willing to teach all who were interested. This is typical of the origin of the expression, "to sit at the feet of a great teacher." It is interesting that this story of Mary and Jesus is the best example we have in the New Testament of someone sitting at Jesus' feet, listening to his teaching. And from the context, Mary was an audience of one. For women to listen in while a rabbi taught the men of a crowd was likely not that unusual. But for a Jewish rabbi to allow a woman to sit at his feet, as his entire audience, was a shocking and even degrading visual symbol.

And then Martha, the head of the household, entered the scene, "distracted by her many tasks," likely the tasks of extending hospitality to an honored teacher. So she went to Jesus and asked, "Do you not care that my sister has left me to do all the work by myself? Tell her then to help me."

Perhaps Martha really did have a lot of chores to do. But I prefer to think she was embarrassed that Mary did not realize a woman's place. The story might have made more sense if Martha had entered the room and asked to have a word in private with Mary. In whispered tone, the older sister could have reminded her, "Come, Mary, you know that the place of a woman is not at the feet of a rabbi. It's not becoming of you, and you are insulting him. You are tiring him for the more important work he has to be about. He came here to rest. He came here asking for our hospitality. Do not take advantage of him. Come to the kitchen with me."

Perhaps Martha knew her sister well enough to know that if she had asked to speak to her in private, it would have done little good. The Rabbi's words had already filled Mary's head, and she would not easily miss this rare opportunity to have Rabbi Jesus to herself. But maybe Martha brought up her concern in front of Jesus to show her respect for him and his need for rest. Yet Jesus defended Mary. "Martha, there is need of only one thing. Mary has chosen the better part, which will not be taken away from her."

Had this rabbi gone mad? Mary had chosen the better part? Woman as learner? Woman sitting alone at the feet of a rabbi? Woman as disciple of a rabbi? In relation to other rabbis, Jesus surely charted his own course in relation to women and others customarily excluded from full participation in the community of faith. He was a different sort of rabbi.

Jesus' Distinctives as a Rabbi

Though similar to other first-century Jewish rabbis, in his relationship to his disciples, in his teaching style, and in legal interpretations, Jesus had his own distinctive style. Note the following:

(1) *The relationship between Jesus and his disciples was permanent, lifelong.* The goal was not for his disciples to take his place, but to remain disciples, not to become rabbis in their own right. Of this New Testament scholar Eduard Schweizer wrote,

> No disciple of Jesus would think of becoming the Son of Man while a Jewish student quite naturally follows his teacher so that later he may become a teacher himself.[18]

(2) *In his teaching, Jesus became more than an interpreter of the Law.* The method of rabbinic teaching was, in the words of Derret,

> to rehearse the student in biblical passages, to explain their meaning, and to rehearse them in the explanation of the meaning. A great

teacher exhausted his text so that no more meaning could be squeezed out of it, and interpretation reached perfection in this way.[19]

Jesus certainly exhibited an impressive respect and mastery of Jewish scripture. But in so many passages, Jesus saw himself not just as interpreting the message, but as embodying the message. The most poignant example of this was his message in Nazareth, "Today, this scripture has been fulfilled in your hearing" (Luke 4:21). It is also clear in Jesus' response to John the Baptist's question of him, "Go and tell John what you have seen and heard. . . . And blessed is anyone who takes no offense at me" (Luke 7:22a, 23).

Jesus lacked the typical reserve of Jewish teachers of his day as they put themselves in the background and scriptural interpretation in the foreground. Because of the Hebraic conviction in God as teacher of the Jewish people, Jesus' personal embodiment of his own message, his blending of messenger and message, was blasphemous to many other rabbis.

(3) *Jesus was not properly schooled as a rabbi.* He lived in a day before the standards of becoming a rabbi had been established. But, still, most rabbis spent years studying in formal schools. Pheme Perkins described this training and Jesus' lack of it.

> Established "schools" had a process by which persons became teachers. They would have to spend years as students or disciples of a famous teacher. An outstanding student would then succeed the master. Others might eventually form their own group. . . . Jesus did not come out of such a school. He had not studied the Law with a famous scribe or been part of a group devoted to interpreting the Scriptures like the Pharisees or Essenes. This fact about Jesus lies behind the question preserved in John 7:15, "How does he know letters, since he has not been taught?" This comment does not imply that Jesus was illiterate. He would have been taught to read the Torah scrolls as well as other forms of reading and writing common in elementary education. But it suggests that Jesus had not been taught how to interpret the Scriptures according to the principles of some school.[20]

(4) *The goal of learning in Jesus' discipling community was not informational but transformational.* The purpose was not the amassing of wisdom, and certainly not the complicated interpretations of scripture. Jesus called his disciples to die to self, to be born from above, to become like little babes. Schweizer said,

> Jesus is not content with precise exegesis of the Law and the various interpretations of it given by the rabbis. He demands radical obedience far transcending mere observance of the letter of the law.[21]

(5) *Jesus obtained his disciples in a different way.* John 1:36 describes how disciples typically sought out their teachers and presented themselves for the learning relationship. Only after careful examination did the rabbi extend an invitation. The caliber of the disciples reflected greatly upon the reputation of the rabbi. Only the brightest and best were accepted. Robbins described this traditional process.

> In rabbinic literature, rabbis are not depicted traveling around as Jesus does to find people who will respond to his summons to become disciple-companions. Instead, the tradition emphasizes the initiative by individual people to receive permission from a rabbi to become one of his student-disciples.[22]

The more familiar pattern for Jesus was his recruiting disciples, seeking them out and calling them to follow him. This would no doubt seem a desperate approach for a rabbi, as if no deserving students would approach him. Unlike others, Jesus called his disciples to come and follow him (Mark 1:16-20).

(6) *Grace was involved in Jesus' call to his disciples.* He did not call the elite, the privileged, the highly respected. "I have not come to call the righteous but sinners to repentance" (Luke 5:32f.). And so Jesus called even the despised, for example, Levi, a tax collector. And in so doing, Jesus broke through the rigidly enforced barriers of the clean and unclean in his society. The radicalness of his invitation is seen in the response of persons, such as Zacchaeus, another tax collector, and in his teaching Mary, a woman.

(7) Jesus' call to discipleship had unprecedented authority. All through the Gospels, people marveled at his authority. The cost of his discipleship was extraordinarily high (Matt 8:19-22), and when Jesus extended the call or spoke as a rabbi, he spoke as if speaking on behalf of God, without apology, without reservation.

As we consider Jesus, the first-century rabbi, we would do well to remember his similarities to and uniquenesses from other rabbis of his day and time.

Jesus as Today's Rabbi

Our focus is not simply upon Jesus as first-century teacher, however, but upon Jesus as the ever-present rabbi for the church today. The teacher he sought to be for the first disciples is the teacher he hopes to be for disciples today. There are at least five reasons why Christians today urgently need to encounter Jesus as ever-present rabbi and teacher:

(1) *Jesus becomes the church's teacher.* I advocate that we refrain from using the title teacher in the church except in referring to Jesus. Jesus advocated this himself when he said,

> But you are not to be called rabbi, for you have one teacher, and you are all students. . . . Nor are you to be called instructors, for you have one instructor, the Messiah. (Matt 23:8, 10)

Those of us engaged in teaching in the church are not the teachers, but rather facilitators of those seeking to encounter the ever-present Rabbi in their lives. Call us enablers or facilitators, and let Jesus be the teacher of the church, then and now! We facilitate encounters with the Teacher and with his teachings. Jesus said, "Take my yoke upon you, and learn from me" (Matt 11:29). He intends to be the church's (his disciples') teacher.

(2) *When the church stops teaching and starts helping people listen and watch for the Rabbi, it changes our posture in relation to the world.* The church has become too protective of its own teachings and too encrusted in its own dogmas and doctrines. It is so heavy-laden with "teaching agenda"—what we want to tell the world—that it prevents others from hearing the voice of the Teacher for themselves. For

too long the world has heard the church, rather than the church's teacher.

While in South Africa in 1992, my wife and I attended a home Bible study sponsored by a local church. The teacher was a young white man, and all the students were black Africans. The Bible study was conducted in a question-"right answer" approach. The leader began by asking the group if they knew the "three reasons Jesus died for our sins." I suspect every person in the group could have identified three reasons why Jesus died for their sins, but the teacher wanted only his reasons and his terminology. The first person to respond gave a very personal reason out of his own experience to which the teacher responded, "Well, that's not the answer I wanted." I watched that young black student recoil, and for the rest of the evening, few in the group ventured responses to his teaching. He began to build an elaborate and complicated theological structure that for him answered every conceivable question. He presented his complete "plan of salvation." Later in the evening, he realized that few in the group had spoken. He complained, saying, "I'm not a monological teacher. I wanted you to ask questions and interact with me, but since you've been so quiet this evening, you have forced me to offer a monologue."

I saw in his behavior too much of the church. When we ask people questions, we are not prepared for their answers, often born of their own experience and unique truth seeking. We want them to use our theological constructs, our terminology. When they do not, we use subtle ways to intimidate or discourage them from pursuing their own questions. The students in that Bible study in South Africa failed to meet and interact with Rabbi Jesus on their own terms and their own ground. Instead, "the church's teacher" got in the way of their interacting with "the Teacher." Japanese theologian Kosuke Koyama aptly described the problem of church teaching:

> Christianity has become so self-righteous that I do not see much future in it. It wants to teach. It does not want to learn. It is arrogant. It is suffering from a "teacher complex." "God, I thank thee that I am not like others, extortioners, unjust, adulterers, or even like this tax collector . . ." There is not much future in this kind of religion.
>
> This religion called Christianity is . . . most interested in teaching people, but not interested in being taught by people. It speaks to people, but it does not listen to them. I do not think Christianity in Asia for the last 400 years has really listened to the people. It has

ignored them. Ignoring things is not so bad, but ignoring people is serious. It has listened to its bishops, theologians, and financial supporters, but it has not listened to the people.[23]

Once when I was in El Salvador, Rev. Carlos Sanchez, then pastor of the Emmanuel Baptist Church of San Salvador, spoke of his experience with Archbishop Oscar Romero. This was at a time of great hostility between Catholics and Protestants, as was the conflict between Romero and his fellow bishops over the proper response to the war. One Sunday the situation was so tense that the archbishop was unable to preach. His bishops were divided against him. Carlos Sanchez had had some contact with the archbishop, and someone who knew this told him privately, "If you want to encourage the archbishop, let him know now."

Carlos organized a secret delegation to visit the archbishop. If other Baptists had learned about this visit, it would have spelled trouble. Indeed, sometime later there was an abortive attempt within the Salvadoran Baptist Association to expel Emmanuel Baptist Church in part because of this visit to the archbishop. Romero also would have been in trouble with the Roman Catholic powers for meeting secretly with Protestants.

When the Baptists met in his private chambers, the archbishop entered the room and said, "Separated brethren, how glad I am to see you!" The term separated brethren is the expression the Roman Catholics use of Protestants in Latin America. The oldest man in the Baptist delegation interrupted him saying, "Excuse me, Father, but we do not feel separated from you."

The archbishop, who presumably was to offer teaching and blessing to all who came to him, was choked with emotion over the old man's statement. Eventually Romero was able to say to them, "I feel more unity with all of you here in this room than with my brother bishops right now." In prayer together, it marked the first time in 400 years of Christianity in El Salvador that such an encounter had ever happened. Two months later, the archbishop was killed.

One might presume that the archbishop was there to teach, but instead, he opened himself to receive and learn. Archbishop Romero surely sensed that the ever-present Teacher was in their midst, in the form of an elderly Baptist. And it was the Teacher who no longer wanted to be separated from him. Our relationship to those who are different from us changes when through them we hear the church's real teacher.

(3) *Discipleship expresses praxis.* First-century rabbis had disciples or followers, and a focus upon Jesus as rabbi is upon ourselves as followers of a teacher. Jesus taught his disciples, and he also sent them "out to proclaim the message, and to have authority to cast out demons" (Mark 3:14b). Therefore, our actions as disciples need also become informed actions, enlightened actions, reflective engagement, praxis. Discipleship expresses praxis, a joining of our thoughts and actions, our ideas and the living out of those ideas. In a church today that too often has the right words but few actions to match those words, or actions that often seem void of theological mandate, to rediscover Jesus as rabbi is to rediscover ourselves as disciples.

The meaning of discipleship today has holistic potential. Saint Francis said, "Preach the gospel at all times; if necessary, use words." In a more modern setting, Frederick Herzog suggested that there is emerging a new way of teaching in which "doctrine arises from discipleship—God-walk rather than God-talk."[24] Discipleship expresses a way of being faithful and acting faithfully that follows the ways of the Rabbi. As Schweizer said, "It was always Jesus who chose the way, filled the days, and put the stamp of his words and deeds on his followers' discipleship."[25] We can achieve praxis through Rabbi Jesus of reflection, words, prayers, and actions.

(4) *We need to rediscover the educational mandate of the church today.* Whatever educational mandate arose from the Sunday School movement of the last century has largely run its course. That is not to say that the Sunday School has no purpose, but classes on Sunday morning are offered in many churches as a way to get people in smaller groupings, linked more intimately to the congregation, as a way to form closer fellowship, or as a way to integrate newcomers. While this is worthy, it does not express a strong educational mandate.

We are overlooking a strong educational mandate in the Gospels. Once discovered, it will provide a biblical rationale and rooting for the teaching and learning that need to occur in the church. Educational techniques and strategies abound, but the church lacks a strong biblical mandate and paradigm for its teaching and learning.

(5) *Prayer can be a time of learning and teaching.* Too often, our prayers are demands or shopping lists we place before God instead of moments of silencing ourselves to wait upon God. We tend to view prayer as pure devotion, not as opportunity for learning from the Teacher. Prayer can be an avenue of dialogue with Rabbi Jesus, just as the first disciples must have prayerfully viewed their time with Jesus. Teachers typically use distance and proximity, questions and answers, struggle and accomplishment as instructional tools. And so, as we interact with the Living Teacher, this relationship might undergird the silences and distances that so often characterize our prayer lives.

Conclusion

In reintroducing Jesus as rabbi, we find that he had much in common with, yet also some qualities distinct from, other rabbis of his day. If we will discover Jesus as a rabbi today, he can become the church's teacher, and that in turn will revolutionize the church, changing its posture to the world, its educational mandate, and the nature and practice of discipleship.

Notes

[1] Howard Clark Kee, *What Can We Know about Jesus?* (Cambridge: Cambridge University Press, 1990) 114.

[2] Marcus J. Borg, *Jesus, a New Vision* (San Francisco: Harper & Row, 1987) 15.

[3] Frederick J. Murphy, *The Religious World of Jesus* (Nashville: Abingdon, 1991) 311.

[4] Bernard J. Lee, S. M., *The Galilean Jewishness of Jesus* (New York: Paulist Press, 1988) 118.

[5] Ibid., 119.

[6] H. L. Ellison, *Dictionary of New Testament Theology,* vol. 3, Colin Brown, ed. (Grand Rapids: Zondervan, 1975) 115-16.

[7] Jaroslav Pelikan, *Jesus Through the Centuries* (New Haven CT: Yale University Press, 1985) 11.

[8] Lee, 120.

[9] Pelikan, 17.

[10] Eduard Schweizer, *Lordship and Discipleship* (Naperville IL: Alec R. Allenson, Inc., 1960) 77.

[11] D. Muller, *Dictionary of New Testament Theology,* vol. 1, Colin Brown, ed. (Grand Rapids: Zondervan, 1971) 484.

[12] Vernon K. Robbins, *Jesus the Teacher* (Philadelphia: Fortress Press, 1984) 87.

[13] Ibid., 117.
[14] Lee, 125-26.
[15] J. Duncan Derrett, *Jesus' Audience* (New York: Seabury Press, 1973) 145.
[16] Lee, 124.
[17] S. Safrai and M. Stern, eds., *Compendium Rerum Iudaicarum ad Novum Testamentum: the Jewish People in the First Century,* vol. 2 (Philadelphia: Fortress Press, 1976) 964-66, passim.
[18] Eduard Schweizer, *Jesus* (Atlanta: John Knox Press, 1971) 40.
[19] Derrett.
[20] Pheme Perkins, *Jesus as Teacher* (Cambridge University Press, 1990) 23.
[21] Schweizer, *Jesus,* 31.
[22] Robbins, 101.
[23] Kosuke Koyama, *Three-Mile-an-Hour God* (Maryknoll NY: Orbis Books, 1979) 51-54.
[24] Frederick Herzog, "A New Spirituality: Shaping Doctrine at the Grass Roots," *Christian Century,* 30 July-6 August, 1986, 680.
[25] Schweizer, *Jesus,* 66.

Chapter 2
Jesus as Charismatic Teacher
John 4:7-15

According to Pheme Perkins, there were three characteristics of a first-century charismatic teacher. He was authoritative, had a charismatic personality, and was an anointed teacher. In this first portrait of Jesus, we sketch him as a charismatic teacher with magnetic appeal that attracted disciples then, as it does today. The appeal came not from his credentials or notoriety, but from his relationship with God.

Surprising Authority

A charismatic teacher does not have the normal status or accepted credentials to be a teacher. Constantly, throughout Jesus' ministry, he was asked, "On whose authority do you speak and act?" Often this was meant as a put-down or insult, because his contemporaries were fully aware that he did not have respected credentials to do what he was doing. He had not studied the law at the feet of the great scholars of his day in order to offer such authoritative interpretations of scripture. Synagogue school as a boy in Nazareth hardly qualified. He had not been recognized by the leading intellectuals to have taught with such authority. He was a charismatic teacher, and this puzzled the people. Where did his authority and learning come from?

In first-century Judaism, there already was an established system of synagogue schools in villages and cities. There was a house of reading, the *bet sefer*. Most male children, even if poor, attended the *bet sefer*, beginning at the age of five or six, to learn to read the Holy Scriptures. At about age eleven, students would move to the *bet talmud*, or house of learning, to study the Mishnah, or oral law. The students would learn to read in Hebrew, though the instruction in the schools was in the everyday vernacular of Aramaic. A few gifted students then would go on to study with master teachers. Perkins points out that of those who did advanced studies,

> Only an upper-class minority had the wealth and leisure to pursue the kind of learning that went on in the more formal school settings of antiquity. Only they could travel to centers like Athens or Jerusalem to hear famous philosophers or teachers of the Law. Only they could pay teachers to come and instruct them, their families, or their associates. Only they could obtain the hand-copied scrolls on which the teachings of the philosophers, the Jewish Scriptures, the commentaries on the Law, the sayings of wise men, the apocalyptic prophesies of the seers, and the like were contained.[1]

As I pointed out in the last chapter, Jesus lived before the time when the standards of becoming a Jewish rabbi had been formally established, so the fact that he had not gone on to study with an advanced teacher did not prevent his acceptance as a rabbi. In John 7:14-17, we read,

> About the middle of the festival Jesus went up into the temple and began to teach. The Jews were astonished at it, saying, "How does this man have such learning, when he has never been taught?" Then Jesus answered them, "My teaching is not mine but his who sent me. Anyone who resolves to do the will of God will know whether the teaching is from God or whether I am speaking on my own."

Note that what surprised the Jewish authorities was not his lack of credentials, but the depth of his wisdom for one who had not received formalized "higher" education.

Throughout his ministry, people were astonished by Jesus. He was a peasant from Galilee. He had not studied under the great teachers nor come from the right family. He was unorthodox in some of his teachings and practices, but he taught so authoritatively.

The chief priests asked him when he was teaching in the temple, "By what authority are you doing these things? Who gave you this authority to do them?" (Mark 11:28). Another time, "the crowds were astounded at his teaching, for he taught them as one having authority, and not as their scribes" (Matt 7:28-29).

Jesus was a charismatic teacher because he did not have a legitimate base of authority. Today, few would argue that Jesus was a great man, a remarkable teacher, a prophet of his day. Jesus only becomes controversial when we try to bring him into the twentieth century. Alive today, he quickly becomes a scandal. As long as he remains a good but dead rabbi, he is acceptable. But if somehow he teaches authoritatively, then what are his credentials? In this era, all one need say is, "Prove it," and his credibility is suspect. Does he have a Ph.D? Is Jesus a graduate of Yale, or Duke, or Harvard, or Cambridge? Has he published a bestselling book, done a university lecture series, or appeared with Oprah or Letterman? Who gave him permission? Who gave him authority?

Color Jesus charismatic, because without the right credentials, he still is an authoritative teacher.

Charismatic Personality

The second feature of Jesus as a teacher is his charisma, his magnetic appeal. It caused a tax collector at a toll booth to leave his oppressive position and follow. It caused those who fished to leave their boats, nets, and father and to follow. Jesus was a charismatic teacher because of the crowds he attracted, because of the anger and devotion he generated.

We know enough about Jesus to gain some sense of his personality. We know something of his humor, his teaching style, his deep sense of resolve, his prayers; and we see his deep feelings in a variety of situations. Jesus reaches us through the power of his personality. It is a personality that seemingly steps out of the pages of the New Testament, just as we are drawn into the characters of a good novel or a captivating movie.

His charismatic personality comes through in the way Jesus interacts with the Samaritan woman at the well (John 4). There is something about the way he approaches her, asking for a drink from her cup. There is something about the way he violates the norms that dictate a man does not talk to a woman in public, a Jew does not drink from a Samaritan's cup, a rabbi does not interact with an adulterous woman, and a Jew does not offer resources of faith to a Samaritan.

The story in John's Gospel says that Jesus stayed behind his disciples at the well because he was "tired out by his journey." But the woman energized him, bringing him back, enlivening his responses. The woman and the rabbi have one of the more fascinating conversations in all of scripture, in part because it should never have happened in the first place. A charismatic teacher breaks the social, religious, moral, and national taboos, setting new boundaries for himself and the woman. His disciples return to the well, shocked and full of questions!

And typical of suspicion that exists between peoples who mistrust one another, the Samaritan woman at first thinks that Jesus is putting down the beliefs of her people. "Are you greater than our ancestor Jacob who gave us (this) well?" Are you making fun of this sacred well, the source of our daily water and communal life?

Jesus says to her, "If you knew the gift of God . . ." Later in the story, the woman recognizes the gift of God and eventually brings a blessing to her people instead of shame. In her rush to share with her people, she leaves her water jar behind at Jesus' feet. The water jar itself is a symbol of the heavy work women had to do, a thankless, back-breaking job of carrying jugs of water from the well some distance to their homes in the city. It was "a woman's job," on behalf of the children, the older people, the men, the sick. Yet when Jesus offered her living water, eternal water, the woman "left her water jar behind and went back to the city" to introduce her neighbors and kin to the rabbi who lifts burdens, who offers living water, who is the Savior, not just of the Jews, but "of the world" (4:42). A charismatic personality lives beyond the expectations of others, and by the magnetism of personality, lifts people beyond burdens, beyond taboos, beyond routines. This woman encountered a charismatic teacher and left her past behind.

Color Jesus with a magnetic personality that drew people to himself, overcoming social taboos and setting them free.

Anointed Teacher

Finally, Jesus experienced a *charism,* or "anointing." Jesus, the charismatic rabbi, was anointed by God, called to a relationship with all who would be his followers. Schweizer said,

> While the disciples walked with Jesus, they were more and more entrusted with a commission and . . . this commission filled lives that were empty, gave purpose to lives frittered away in daily routine, gave meaning to lives condemned to be meaningless.[2]

The goal of a first-century rabbi was to establish a name for himself so that prospective disciples would come and present themselves as candidates. A rabbi would carefully interview and screen candidates so that his disciples would truly be an honor to him. The stature of a rabbi was in large part determined by the impressiveness of his disciples.

Jesus was a charismatic teacher, compelled by his own deep sense of calling. He went out to the byways and highways and called the most unworthy and unlikely persons as his disciples. There's grace, not merit, in Jesus' call to his disciples then, and now. "Anyone who resolves to do the will of God" (John 7:17a) is my disciple. And when this charismatic teacher said, "anyone," he meant anyone.

Color Jesus as a person anointed with a calling, a person calling others, not on the basis of their merit but on the basis of need.

Conclusion

Jesus as charismatic teacher was so unorthodox that he did not need nor require permission or endorsement from the world. His mandate as teacher came from God alone. By strength of his charismatic personality, he empowered others to step beyond the social taboos and hear his liberating words. He was anointed with a mandate to call others to discipleship—the unworthy, the unnoticed, the unlikely.

Today, persons might be attracted to a charismatic teacher if they struggle with Jesus' legitimacy or authority, or need a more personal and human connection to Jesus, or lack a sense of calling from the one called of God.

Prayer is envisioning the one whom we cannot see. The Rabbi of the first century still has much to teach us and stands before us as our teacher. Do you have the vision to paint a picture of the Charismatic Rabbi, using the bold colors, sharp features, and magnetic draw it would require?

Notes

[1] Pheme Perkins, *Jesus as Teacher* (Cambridge: Cambridge University Press, 1990) 121.

[2] Eduard Schweizer, *Jesus* (Atlanta: John Knox Press, 1971) 41.

Chapter 3
Jesus as Subversive Sage
John 12:1-8

History tends to be recorded by those who have the means to be literate, those who have the resources to write and store books, and those who have the power to convince others that their interpretation of events is "correct." Members of the dominant class have the power to convince persons not in power that their dominant perspective is the correct one, the divine way, thus resulting in oppression. Indeed, the history of any society is usually written and recorded by the dominant class. Certainly this has been true in the United States. History for us typically means history from the white male perspective. The accomplishments of women, African-Americans, or Native Americans have rarely been acknowledged in our history books.

Just as most modern history has been recorded from a dominant perspective, the majority of the Hebrew wisdom writings were written by and have been retained largely by the upper class. Even so, they are a rich treasure of wisdom, found mostly in Job, Ecclesiastes, and Proverbs. In Proverbs 4:7-8a, we read, "The beginning of wisdom is this: Get wisdom, and whatever else you get, get insight. Prize her highly, and she will exalt you."

Seeking wisdom is a human universal. All religions depend upon wisdom in one form or another. Wisdom is a kind of knowing that comes from reflection upon our experiences. Those who engage in such reflection over many years usually become wise; they learn from their mistakes and see their successes in context.

In ancient Israel, wisdom was taught by teachers of wisdom in special schools.[1] These teachers were called sages, and their writings reflected great wisdom. In the New Jerusalem Bible, the opening verses of the apocalyptic wisdom book of Ecclesiasticus state:

> All wisdom comes from the Lord, she is with him forever. . . . From whom has the root of wisdom ever been uncovered? Her resourceful ways, who knows them? One only is wise, terrible indeed, seated on his throne, the Lord. It was he who created, inspected, and weighed (wisdom) up, and then poured her out on all his works. (1:1, 6-9)

Much of Jewish wisdom writing is found in the form of proverbs. The proverbs of Israel's wisdom writing were short, easily memorized sentences intended for oral instruction.

> Parents taught them to their children . . . and the name "son" is retained when master teaches pupil, since the sages ran schools. "Wisdom" became a privilege of the educated and therefore lettered classes.[2]

The wisdom literature of Hebrew scriptures was "somewhat upper class and not really for the masses. The most of it pertains to the leisure class."[3] Ecclesiasticus, written less than 200 years before Christ, speaks of wisdom's home with the elite.

> Leisure gives the scribe the chance to acquire wisdom; a man with few commitments can grow wise. How can the ploughman become wise, whose sole ambition is to wield the goad, driving his oxen, engrossed in their work, his conversation limited to bullocks, his thoughts absorbed in the furrows he traces and his long evenings spent in fattening heifers? Similarly with all workmen and craftsmen, toiling day and night. . . . All these people rely on their hands, and each is wise at his own craft. . . . But you will not find them in the parliament, they do not hold high rank in the assembly. . . . and they do not meditate on the Law. They are not remarkable for their culture or judgment, nor are they found frequenting philosophers. . . . Not so with the one who concentrates his mind and his meditation on the Law of the Most High. He researches into the wisdom of all the ancients, he occupies his time with the prophecies. . . . He researches into the hidden sense of proverbs, he ponders the obscurities of parables. (38:24-27, 31, 33; 39:1, 3 NJB)

The assumption of this writer reflects the simplicity and naiveté the privileged writer wanted to see in farmers, craftpersons, and peasants. Yet, it is a serious mistake to assume peasants were disinterested in wisdom. Proverbs actually developed through folk tradition long before written wisdom was compiled. "While the great collections of wisdom were being compiled, popular wisdom flowed on unabated."[4] The influence of this popular wisdom is evident in the Gospel traditions.

Wisdom Teacher

Jesus, like sages down through the centuries, frequently stated his wise sayings as proverbs. Borg gave this explanation about Jesus' use of proverbs:

> The sayings of Jesus include many memorable one- or two-liners: "No one can serve two masters"; "A city set on a hill cannot be hid"; "No one lights a lamp and hides it under a bushel." (There are over 100 proverbs in the sayings of Jesus.) Some of these may have been freshly coined by Jesus himself; many may already have been traditional proverbs. In either case, to a large extent they expressed truisms; indeed their power depended upon the immediate way in which they made sense, their evident truthfulness. . . . Like the sages of the Old Testament, Jesus often pointed to nature as a source of insight. "Consider the lilies of the field; they neither toil nor spin." The observation could take the form of a question: "Are grapes gathered from thorn bushes, or figs from thistles?" The appeal to the intelligence is clear: "Of course not," is the obvious answer. The similar saying, "A good tree bears good fruit," makes an equally common-sense observation.[5]

Jesus not only made use of proverbs, he stood strongly within the overall Jewish wisdom tradition. According to *Harper's Bible Dictionary,* some of his parables (for example, the house built on rock or sand, and the tower) are similar to the themes found in the Old Testament wisdom books of Job, Proverbs, and Ecclesiastes.[6]

> There are identifiable sixteen "wisdom parables" of Jesus, which he taught informally in the open, or in the home of a learner (Mark 2:15-22), or at the tables of Pharisees (Luke 11:37-54). Time and again the ancient proverbial wisdom of his people appeared in his practical teaching: "A city that is set on a hill cannot be hid" (Matt 5:14); "Take no thought for the morrow" (Matt 6:34); "Those who are well have no need of a physician" (Matt 9:12 RSV). Jesus the sage was exalted by Paul to the point of being considered wisdom personified; he was "the wisdom of God," "our wisdom" (1 Cor 1:24, 30); in him were hidden "the treasures of wisdom and knowledge" (Col 2:3). The author of the Gospel of John equates Jesus with the Logos, a Greek concept of "the Word" not entirely unrelated to the personified Jewish wisdom. The Epistle of James also embodies wisdom concepts.[7]

The Gospels speak of Jesus' wisdom more than we may realize. As a boy, "The child grew and became strong, filled with wisdom; and the favor of God was upon him" (Luke 2:40). Again, "Jesus increased in wisdom and in years" (Luke 2:52). When Jesus returned as an adult to his hometown, the people said of him, "What is this wisdom that has been given to him?" (Mark 6:2). Jesus, sending out his disciples, said, "Be wise as serpents" (Matt 10:16b). Jesus called himself the child of wisdom personified (Luke 7:35). He was indeed a teacher (and learner) of wisdom.

Subversive Teacher

Jesus reflected use of what Marcus Borg labels as subversive or skeptical wisdom, although he was not the first in Jewish history to criticize the conventional wisdom of the dominant class. According to Borg,

> In the Hebrew Bible, the authors of Ecclesiastes and Job protested against the conventional wisdom represented by the book of Proverbs, that easy confidence that the righteous would prosper and the wicked wither. They were subversive sages who challenged and subverted the popular wisdom of their day. Jesus stood in this tradition of subversive wisdom. He used the forms of wisdom to subvert conventional ways of seeing. His proverbs and parables often reversed ordinary perception, functioning to jolt his hearers out of their present "world," their present way of seeing reality. The content of his teaching also subverted the world of conventional wisdom.[8]

That Jesus was a peasant and his ministry was largely directed to peasants is beyond debate. He was a rural Galilean Jew, which is just another way of saying "peasant," and he had no formal advanced learning. He was a part of the permanent "under" class. He was reminded of this often. "Is this man not from Galilee?" (John 7:41, 52), people asked incredulously. They set him apart by his folksy Galilean accent (Matt 26:74).

Jesus was subversive in part because he taught from an early Jewish peasant's perspective. Compare the differences between the following teachings of Jesus and the proverbs from Hebrew Scripture:

Blessed are you who are poor, for yours in the kingdom of God. (Luke 6:20a)	The wealth of the rich is their fortress; the poverty of the poor is their ruin. (Prov 10:15)
Blessed are you who are hungry now, for you shall be filled. (Luke 6:21a)	Better to be despised and have a servant, than to be self-important and lack food. (Prov 12:9)
When you give a banquet, invite the poor, the crippled, the lame, and the blind. And you will be blessed. (Luke 14:13-14a)	The poor are disliked even by their neighbors, but the rich have many friends. (Prov 14:20)
How hard it is for those who have wealth to enter the kingdom of God. Indeed, it is easier for a camel to go through the eye of a needle than for someone who is rich to enter the kingdom of God. (Luke 18:24b-25)	Misfortune pursues sinners, but prosperity rewards the righteous. (Prov 13:21)
Jesus looked up and saw rich people putting their gifts into the treasury; he also saw a poor widow put in two small copper coins. He said, "Truly, I tell you, this poor widow has put in more than all of them." (Luke 21:1-3)	Many seek the favor of the generous, and everyone is a friend to a giver of gifts. (Prov 19:6)
I have come to call not the righteous but sinners to repentance. (Luke 5:32)	The rich rules over the poor, and the borrower is the slave of the lender. (Prov 22:7)

Clearly Jesus reflected peasant wisdom, a rare look at the more popular wisdom of his day. And of course, coming from the lower class of society, it challenged the assumptions of the more dominant wisdom. It was not wisdom that the rich people had taught "their poor people" to repeat. It was subversive wisdom. It subverted the wisdom that dominated the many to benefit the few.

Jesus himself seemed to recognize this subversive role:

> I thank you, Father, Lord of heaven and earth, because you have hidden these things from the wise and the intelligent and have revealed them to the infants; yes, Father, such was your gracious will. (Matt 11:25-26)

The apostle Paul recognized as much when he wrote to the church at Corinth, "Yet among the mature we do speak wisdom, though it is not a wisdom of this age or of the rulers of this age" (1 Cor 2:6). Paul asked,

> Where is the one who is wise? Where is the scribe? Where is the debater of this age? Has not God made foolish the wisdom of the world? For since, in the wisdom of God, the world did not know God through wisdom, God decided, through the foolishness of our proclamation, to save those who believe.... For God's foolishness is wiser than human wisdom.... God chose what is foolish in the world to shame the wise. (1 Cor 1:20-21, 25a, 27a).

Jesus was a typical Jewish sage, a part of the tradition of Jewish wisdom teachers. Yet he represented the skeptical part of that tradition, and in him we may have preserved a rare example of wisdom from the Jewish under-class perspective.

Subversive Sage

The strokes of this portrait of Jesus as subversive sage emerge from a scene in Bethany when Mary anointed Jesus' head with expensive burial ointment and Judas protested her extravagance. I have always been taken back at the words of Jesus: "You always have the poor with you." Judas had a point! "Why was this perfume not sold ... and the money given to the poor?" (John 12:5). Jesus himself gave the same advice when he responded to the rich young ruler, "Go, sell your possessions, and give the money to the poor, and you will have treasure in heaven" (Mark 10:21).

Yet, one of the things that those of dominant class most enjoy is critiquing the way poor people use their resources: "Why does that woman use food stamps to buy such an expensive cut of meat? Why do they buy cigarettes? Why do they drive such expensive cars?"

But in this text we have to remember that this is a peasant rabbi speaking to and with his own, not a middle class person reflecting upon the poor from a comfortable distance. Jesus, the peasant-rabbi, was saying, "My kind and my people will be with you always. But as for me personally, I do not have much longer."

Jesus' compassion and identity with the poor is evidenced more in Mark's version of this incident, "For you always have the poor with you, and you can show kindness to them whenever you wish; but you will not always have me" (Mark 14:7). Jesus saw himself as being sent to preach "good news to the poor" (Luke 4:18), but this involves something far greater than a handout by the haves to the have-nots. It involves recognizing the integrity and wisdom of the poor.

In Mark's account of this incident, Jesus, the wise sage, sums up the meaning of what Mary has done for him, saying, "Truly I tell you, wherever the good news is proclaimed in the whole world, what she has done will be told in remembrance of her" (Mark 14:9).

Why would Mary's anointing of Jesus be told "wherever the good news is proclaimed"? Was it not because of the insight Mary exhibited? Quietly, without words, she recognized Jesus' approaching death. Maybe even before Jesus was willing to admit or to verbalize it, Mary prepared a healthy man for death as if he was already dead. Why anoint a living man with burial ointments?

Only a very wise or an utterly foolish woman would do such a thing. Mary saw the bigger picture of what Jesus and his disciples were working against. She knew what societies always do to subversive sages. She was not so caught up in the hysteria over her brother's resurrection that she missed seeing where Jesus was headed. By the Gospel accounts, Mary was the first of all the disciples to see Jesus' approaching death. The rest of the disciples could not see it, even the night Jesus was arrested. As Jesus was taking leave of the disciples at his last supper, Peter asked him, "Lord where are you going? Why can I not follow you?" (John 13:36a, 37b). At the earlier meal in Bethany, Mary understood and ritualized it by anointing Jesus' body with burial ointments while he was still living. And the disciples were aghast!

They scolded Mary. I think they were not concerned just about the cost, but about how morbid Mary was acting. If Jesus was to die, what meaning was left for their lives?

Perhaps Mary had the wisdom to see through her brother's resurrection that Jesus' death, as painful as it would be, would not mean the end of her following him. Jesus had said to Mary's family when he raised Lazarus from the dead, "Those who believe in me, even though they die, will live" (John 11:25b). And if it happened to her brother, why not also to Jesus?

In effect, Jesus was saying, "Yes, giving alms to the poor is important. But sometimes the poor need more than our alms. Sometimes we need to recognize their wisdom. Mary has been so wise. This is not the time to scold her but to lift up her wise example for all the world to see. Wisdom dwells in surprising places, even among us poor, even within our women. Rather than giving gifts to the poor, this is a time when we need to recognize the gift this peasant woman has given us."

Color Jesus a subversive sage, his sturdy head dripping with burial ointments, his disciples standing around aghast, a wise peasant woman beside him, demonstrating that God's wisdom subverts our prejudices and assumptions and turns dominant thinking upside down.

Conclusion

We too have conventional and subversive wisdom in our society. God's wisdom tends to subvert society's conventional wisdom. God's wisdom tends to be more obvious to those marginalized, and less so to the comfortable. For this reason, the Subversive Sage can be a most discomforting and threatening teacher. Or the Sage can be seen as the source of liberation for both oppressed and oppressor, subverting the captive way things are into God's liberating ways.

Notes

[1] Marcus Borg, *Jesus, a New Vision* (San Francisco: Harper & Row, 1988) 124.

[2] "Introduction to the Wisdom Books," the *New Jerusalem Bible* (New York: Doubleday, 1985) 751.

[3] *The Interpreter's Dictionary of the Bible,* vol. 4 (Nashville: Abingdon, 1962) 856.

[4] *New Jerusalem Bible.*

[5] Marcus Borg, *Jesus, a New Vision* (San Francisco: Harper & Row, 1987) 98.

[6] Madeleine S. Miller and J. Lane Miller, *Harper's Bible Dictionary* (New York: Harper & Row, 1973) 524.

[7] Ibid., 818.

[8] Borg, 115.

*I express my appreciation to Dr. Grant Ward for many of the ideas about subversive wisdom expressed in this section. Dr. Grant is an Old Testament scholar living in Philadelphia, and shared his insights with me in personal conversation.

Chapter 4
Jesus as Transforming Teacher
Mark 3:31-35

Perhaps we should be upset with Jesus about this. When Jesus' mother and brothers and sisters were outside his house asking to see him, why would he say, "Who are my mother and brothers and sisters?" What kind of impertinent son would say such a thing? Won't people forever misread Jesus' statement as implying that family no longer matters?

In reality, family and parentage were of no small concern to a first-century Jew. One's family obligation held a primacy in one's life. There existed Eastern values regarding one's ancestry, parentage, and lineage.

Mark locates Jesus "at home" in Capernaum (2:1). This is the town by the Sea of Galilee where Simon, Andrew, James, and John lived (1:29). Jesus had been healing and teaching with so much authority and with such a popular response that he "could no longer go into a town openly, but stayed out in the country, and people came to him from every quarter" (1:45).

Apparently, when Jesus finally did quietly slip into Capernaum, it was not long after that "it was reported that he was at home. So many gathered around that there was no longer room for them, not even in the front of the door" (2:1-2). Then the story is told of the four friends who cut a hole in the roof of the house reported to be Jesus' "home" so that Jesus could heal their paralytic friend.

At this early point in his Gospel, Mark reports after another Sabbath healing inside the synagogue that "the Pharisees went out and immediately conspired with the Herodians against him, how to destroy him" (3:6). Matters were tensing up.

Crowds came from everywhere.

> They came to him in great numbers from Judea, Jerusalem, Idumea, beyond the Jordan, and the region around Tyre and Sidon. Jesus told his disciples to have a boat ready for him because of the crowd, so that they would not crush him; for he had cured many, so that all who had diseases pressed upon him to touch him. (vv. 8b-10)

Jesus then went up a mountain and "called to him those whom he wanted," and he "appointed twelve, whom he also named apostles, to be with him, and to be sent out to proclaim the message and to have authority to cast out demons" (3:13-15). Mark seems to suggest that the twelve were appointed and empowered because the anxious crowds were getting out of control, pressing in on Jesus to the point where he was personally worried about getting crushed.

After appointing and empowering these disciples, once again Jesus "went home." We presume this meant to his home in Capernaum, "and the crowd came together again" around his house, "so that they could not even eat." Another time, Mark reports that Jesus brought his apostles to a lonely place because "they had no leisure even to eat" (6:31). At home in Capernaum, there was no room to eat.

Now Mark reports this utterly curious, little-noticed response by Jesus' family. "When his family heard it, they went out to restrain him, for people were saying, 'He has gone out of his mind.' " (3:21). Other translators say, his family went to Capernaum "to take charge of him" (NIV), or, "they set out to take charge of him" (NJB, REB). And the scribes "who had come down from Jerusalem said, 'He is possessed by Beelzebul,' and, 'He drives out demons by the prince of demons' " (3:22 REB). They thought Jesus was demon-possessed!

What was a family to do, when one of their own had such charges made against him? What was a family to do when an adult member of the family was acting in such a way that everyone was talking about him? What was a poor Nazarene mother to do when the elders of the nation came all the way from the capital to question her son's sanity?

It was time to set out and intervene. It was time for a mother's talk with her son. It was time to gather up the sane children, those around whom there were no rumors, and have a family meeting.

> Then his mother and brothers came; and standing outside they sent to him and called him. A crowd was sitting around him; and they said to him, "Your mother and your brothers and sisters are outside, asking for you." And he replied, "Who are my mother and my brothers?" And looking around at those who sat around him, he said, "Here are my mother and my brothers. Whoever does the will of God is my brother and sister and mother." (3:31-35)

How would you like to be the one sent out to the street to give this message: "Woman, you came because you heard your son was insane"? How do you tell a mother, "Your son doesn't even recognize who you are," or, "Your son has just disowned you"?

The Change Agent

"Who are my mother and brother and sister?" Maybe Paul provides the answer. "So if anyone is in Christ, there is a new creation: everything old has passed away; see, everything has become new! All this is from God" (2 Cor 5:17-18a). This is the God who says, "See, I am making all things new!" (Rev 21:5a).

I don't think Jesus meant disrespect for his family. Rather, he was talking about transformation. When the transforming power of God takes ahold of us, we are changed persons. The relationships and struggles we had before, those things that took power over us, will never again be the same.

Did Jesus' blood relatives come to him because they were concerned about the rumors? Did his family of origin come because they were concerned about their good name, or because neighbors and friends had told them, "You'd better go and straighten things out"?

Clearly Jesus was not on the same wavelength as his brothers, sisters, and mother. Their concerns were not the same. I remember my parents often joking with one another about their families of origins and about the way each did things differently from my immediate family. Jesus was at a new place with his chosen "family," and not at the same place as his Nazarene kin.

Mary and her other children likely went to Capernaum because they no longer recognized Jesus. He was not acting as he had when he lived with them. Something had taken hold of him. They went because, compared with how they had known him, he was acting crazy, like someone possessed. Indeed, something had taken hold of him.

This story from Mark's Gospel may correct our view of Jesus as someone who was born into perfection. Rather, we see in his birth someone intended to take on the role of Savior of the world, someone destined by God even in his birth.

But growing up, he was just a boy of Nazareth, a carpenter's son. "Is not this Jesus, the son of Joseph, whose father and mother we know? How can he now say (these things)?" (John 6:42). The people who had known him before, his own family, no longer recognized him. They had come to Capernaum to "take charge of him, to restrain him." It was time to bring him back to his old self, back under family authority. So Mary went, likely as a widow, taking with her Jesus' brothers and sisters.

Jesus had changed. But change is not a very effective word in this context. Transformed is a much stronger word in English. Jesus had experienced the transforming power of God in his life, and his family no longer recognized him. Those who had known him before knew him no longer.

That is what happens with transformation. "All things" for Jesus had been made new. He was now the agent of transformation, making people new. The lame were walking. The blind were seeing. The deaf were hearing. Those tormented with inner voices and possessed with uncontrollable powers were talking rationally. Those thrown about with seizures and fits were calm. The lepers were no longer shunned, for they had clear skin. Something had fundamentally changed.

You and I cannot accomplish or control transformation. We cannot transform ourselves or others. We can invite others to transformation. We can walk with and encourage others through transforming seasons of their lives. But there is only one transforming power in this universe, only one who has the power to take hold of someone and make them unrecognizable to their families.

I can effect all kinds of cosmetic changes on myself. I can rearrange the mental, emotional, or volitional "furniture" within me. But I cannot take the "old me" and turn myself into the "new me." I can only make myself receptive and ready. I can move as I sense the divine change agent moving within and among me.

Personal Testimony

If my family of origin was to be introduced to me today, after a separation of twenty years, they would surely not recognize me. I am in such a different place. I think differently. I believe differently. I respond differently. I hope for different things now. Different things engage me. I live for different reasons. Is it my doing? Was it my choosing? In my case, I can say absolutely not.

I was four years out of seminary, four years into my first pastoral position, all the while believing that preaching was a dated relic of the past. I would have preferred to get everyone into small sharing groups.

More than twenty years ago, when I entered my first position as an educational pastor, I was not seen as a preacher by others, not believing in it myself. I did not become a pastor because of a long line of pastors in my ancestry or because I grew up with pastors as my heroes. I don't know how far back you'd have to go on either side of my family to find a pastor, and one person whom I least respected during my growing up years was my pastor! How did it happen that I am now a preacher and pastor?

In my experience, it was largely the transforming power of God upon my life. It was the Transforming Teacher who helped me bit by bit, who walked with me step by step, who stayed with me day by day, until the transforming power of God began to take hold. That angry nineteen-year-old young man who once said, "I've never yet met a pastor I could trust," who had no use for preaching nor the organized church, now can say, "But for the grace of God, I today am proud to be a pastor, delighted to be in a ministry of preaching, and find my surest home in the church." I don't know how I got from A to B, I only know I couldn't have, wouldn't have, done it of my own accord.

I continue to experience God's transforming power. When I was in San Salvador several years ago, I went to the chapel where Archbishop Oscar Romero was killed. I was inexplicably overcome with a sense of emotion. Finding a quiet place around the corner in the chapel, I got down on the kneeling bench and became ever more fully in touch with my own sinfulness. Shaking with emotion, several questions bombarded me: Why did Jesus have to die? And why did this saintly Romero have to die, here, in this place? Surely for no other reason than that I did not care enough, love enough, nor risk enough to keep it from happening. Wiping my eyes and clearing my throat, a deep insight came to me. I realized not how horrible I had been, but how forgiven I am and how fresh and new is my calling from God. Something from beyond had happened. Defying explanation, the Teacher had come to me.

At moments like that, I get up off my knees and suddenly discover that I can see where before I was blind. I can hear where before I was deaf. I can walk where before I was lame. I can be calm where before I was seized with fear.

I will never forget coming home from my first overseas family sabbatical in 1984. We had never before lived in the third world. We found our transition to home painful. The Teacher had had a hand upon us while we were away, and we had been transformed. We weren't sure whether people back home would recognize us, or that we would recognize ourselves or our former values or lifestyle. Things would be different. Risk was involved.

Transformation and Risk

Are you taking risks today that you did not believe in ten years ago? Are you engaged in a vocation or life change that you never would have chosen a few years back? Are the things that engage you, that make you angry, that you respond to different today than in an earlier time in your life? Is your language different today than it was ten years ago?

How many little girls who were taught, "You can't do this," are now doing it? How many little children who were abused have now learned to love themselves? How many maturing youth who, by their insecurity, used to blame everyone else are now taking responsibility for their own lives? How many men who used to be afraid of making commitments or taking risks are now known by their commitments and risks? How many little boys who were taught to be tough are now vulnerable and caring? How many adults who once never knew how to trust others are now reliable partners? How many women who once were afraid are now overcoming their fears and claiming new places for themselves? How many Christians, once quiet and withdrawn, are now leaders in their community of faith?

We must not be as interested in informed Christians as we are in transformed Christians. Becoming a Christian is not a slow, evolutionary process in which a young person eventually "ends up a Christian." Nor is it when one finally "knows enough" or "understands enough." The call of the gospel is for *metanoia,* or to change one's way of being. It calls for revolutionary, not evolutionary, change.

Jesus launched his ministry calling for radical repentance (Mark 1:15). When he was asked to form an analogy of the kind of change he was calling for, he went to the most radical image of all. It is like being born all over again (John 3:7f.), like becoming a newborn child, except this time you are not born in the love of your mother's womb but born from above, born from your heavenly mother's love. We become what God intends us to be, not by a simple one-time decision on our part, but by radical transformation, by turnaround experiences that happen again and again throughout our lifetimes.

This is the portrait of Jesus as transforming teacher. What Jesus offers speaks to our hungers, our needs, our brokenness. It speaks to that which seems so insurmountable, and offers us the transforming power of God. Those who once knew us no longer recognize us. We become transformed.

In a wonderful Canadian film entitled, *Jesus of Montreal,* an actor-director is asked by a Catholic priest to "freshen up" the passion play that has been produced at a hilltop monastery in the city of Montreal for many years. When this actor-director begins to do research on the life of Christ, and then recruits an unorthodox acting troupe, something begins to overtake them as they perform the passion story for others. The story itself is transformed. It is no longer about something that happened "back then." The ancient story becomes intertwined into their stories, to the point where they themselves are the passion story. They find themselves transformed. They relate to one another as transformed persons. Their lives become as scandalous and tragic and fulfilled as did those of Jesus and his first disciples.

Jesus as transforming teacher teaches us to sit at the feet of the Rabbi; to come with our own disabilities, hurts, and brokenness; to come seeking transformation; to come believing that it can happen to us. We must be willing to engage the Teacher, to push the Teacher and push ourselves until we can see our path clearly. We must learn to be receptive, discerning, and intuitive. We must be willing to allow the Teacher and the Teacher's disciples to support us as we claim what God has laid before us. But how can we know whether the transformation is of God or of ourselves or of natural life circumstances?

Discerning the Transforming Power

Mainline Protestants and many Catholics may find the language of transformation difficult. To say of oneself, "I've been transformed," may seem smug, presumptuous, or arrogant. If all change that happens to us is not necessarily the result of the Transforming Teacher, how, then, can we determine whether the change is "of God" or of our own doing?

Most of us know incidents, either in our own lives or as we observe others, when self-serving change was arrogantly credited to God. And most of us likely have been around people who attributed all of life's happenings and results to God. How can we know when change is truly the result of an encounter with the Transforming Teacher? Discernment, or rightly interpreting our lives, is at issue.

Many people are quite hesitant to identify transformations in their lives. They do not want to seem presumptuous with God or speak of God's involvement so casually as to disrespect the divine mystery. Yet, if we are honest, there are times when our hesitancy is due to our cowardice and fear.

There are times in our lives as persons of faith when the imprint of God is evident, if we but have eyes to recognize it. When we are reluctant to speak of these moments with others, then our discernment remains private and reclusive. Lacking feedback from others, private discernment becomes inevitably distorted. We are robbed even of the insight from hearing ourselves speak aloud about things that come from deep within us.

Communal discernment is that mutual opportunity to share with others to gain their feedback and response. It is the most effective check against private distortions. Only as we have the prayerful and honest response from others who are also engaged in discernment around their own lives can we begin to speak with confidence about our encounters with the Transforming Teacher.

Theologian Leonard I. Sweet explains how he has learned to discern God's direction in life events.

> I used to put almost everything down to happenstance, coincidence, being in the right place at the right time.... But two scholars have helped me to see the hand of God more visibly in the events of our lives. Carl Jung['s] ... concept of "synchronicity" suggests that what we call "coincidence" is often the coming together of events that really belong together. John B. Cobb, Jr., ... contends that there is a "directivity" tugging at the heart of human experience that prompts the "synchronicity." There is a divine gravity pulling all living things toward a fresh future with new possibilities and grand surprises. Much of who we are depends on who we choose to become, and these choices take place within the context of circumstances that appear random, but are really the Spirit's "synchronicity" closing some doors and opening others.[1]

Frederick Buechner is one of those writers for whom discernment of transformation has brought forth unique autobiographical insight. In *Now and Then,* he wrote,

> There is no event so commonplace but that God is present within it, always hiddenly, always leaving you room to recognize him or not to recognize him, but all the more fascinatingly because of that, all the more compellingly and hauntingly....
>
> Listen to your life. See it for the fathomless mystery that it is. In the boredom and pain of it no less than in the excitement and gladness: touch, taste, smell your way to the holy and hidden heart of it because in the last analysis all moments are key moments and life itself is grace.[2]

In another context Buechner wrote,

> The question is not whether the things that happen to you are chance things or God's things because, of course, they are both at once. There is no chance thing through which God cannot speak.... The words he speaks are incarnate in the flesh and blood of ourselves and of our own footsore and sacred journeys. We cannot live our lives constantly looking back, listening back, lest we be turned to pillars of longing and regret, but to live without listening at all is to live deaf to the fullness of the music. Sometimes we avoid listening for fear of what we may hear, sometimes for fear that we may hear nothing at all but the empty rattle of our own feet on the pavement. But ... "be not afraid, ... for lo, I am with you always, even unto the end of the world." He says he is with us on our journeys. He says he has been with us since each of our journeys began. Listen for him. Listen to the sweet and bitter airs of your present and your past for the sound of him.[3]

Both Sweet and Buechner would affirm that discernment is an autobiographical activity involving seeing God's story in our stories.

Conclusion

Paint the portrait of Jesus the Transforming Teacher, where a neat boundary cannot be traced between Jesus the Healer and Jesus the Teacher. The one who teaches and the one who heals is the one who holds God's transforming power and offers it freely to us, and to the world.

God intervenes in our lives through the presence of the Transforming Teacher. We need the courage to speak of that intervention and presence with respect, to share our discernments communally and prayerfully so as to let them be heard aloud and gain correcting and affirming responses. We must learn to depend upon these transformations and act upon them as signs of God's calling. "Everything old has passed away; see, everything has become new! All this is from God!"

Notes

[1] Leonard I. Sweet, *New Life in the Spirit* (Philadelphia: Westminister Press, 1982) 69-70.

[2] Frederick Buechner, *Now and Then* (San Francisco: Harper & Row, 1983) 87.

[3] Frederick Buechner, *The Sacred Journey* (San Francisco: Harper & Row, 1982) 77-78.

Chapter 5
Jesus as Lover of Questions
Matthew 15:21-28

The church today often appears frightened of questions. We cloak ourselves in dogma and creed or in confessional and theological statements so as to leave no question unanswered. Indeed, many churches experiencing explosive growth in our society offer "pat" answers. Their preachers say, "I know the answers, and if you'll let me, I'll give them to you! Receive my answers, and you will be saved!"

So many people are frantic for a human being in whom they can place ultimate trust. They crave for a level of certainty that only an "answers religion" can provide. They believe in a transposed faith, one in which answers that may have emerged in one person's faith-walk are transposed onto others who have entirely different questions. Transposed answers are not the result of struggle from within, but are grafted from without. There are too many churches whose primary message is: "You don't question!" A church or pastor who does not have all the answers is perceived as vacillating and weak of faith.

We Americans are typically rough on questions. We have little respect for questions. We prefer the "quick answer." We seem unable to tolerate uncertainty. The in-between times drive us crazy. We would rather tear into a question, rip it apart, and settle for the first superficial answer, and then cling to that with everything we have. Our quick answer must be an unchanging truth.

So many disillusioned people in our society today have given up on the church because of that mentality. They were told their preacher or church had all the answers. And the first time when life handed them something their easy answers did not address, their faith and confidence in God just as easily fell apart. They walked away, intending never to return.

Jesus loved questions! That might sound odd to our ears, but it is hard to reach any other conclusion after studying the four Gospels. The Greek word, *erotao,* which means "to ask a question or inquire," is used 49 times in the Gospels. Another Greek word, *eperotao,* meaning "to ask," is as common in the Gospels, appearing 52 times. In Luke,

Jesus asked 89 teaching questions; in Matthew, 85; and in Mark, 47. If you read his teaching narratives, you encounter one question after another.

Jesus' Questioning Technique

Jesus often answered questions with a question. "Just then a lawyer stood up to test Jesus. 'Teacher,' he said, 'what must I do to inherit eternal life?' He said to him, 'What is written in the law? What do you read there?' " (Luke 10:25-26). If you read through the Gospel of Mark, for example, you will encounter only a few occasions when Jesus did not answer the challenging questions of other lawyers and teachers with a question. On eleven different occasions in that Gospel, he answered their questions with a question. And typically, he did not explain himself when those in his audience were puzzled. He left them with their questions.

Jesus was known for his parables, which he also rarely explained to the crowds. What is a parable told but a question asked? Those who heard Jesus' parables surely asked themselves, "What does this parable mean? Why did he tell this story to me?" The real artistry of a first-century rabbi was as much in the ability to frame questions as to answer them. Jesus disarmed as many detractors with questions as with answers.

Jesus loved questions! He not only answered his challengers with questions; he loved asking questions of his followers. If Jesus had not been allowed to ask questions, much of his teaching would have been silenced.

Marie Livingston Roy described Jesus' unique questioning technique.

> Jesus showed an unerring ability to ask the penetrating question. With a word, he exposed the pettiness of spirit that prevented persons from receiving the fullness of life he offered. Glimpsing truth face to face, they were stripped of pretense, self-conceit, hypocrisy. Some people welcomed the kingdom, freely accepting their place in it; others found the cost too hard to bear and turned away. Regardless of their response, they had each encountered God in the questions of Jesus.[1]

Certainly, the passage that describes Jesus' interaction with the Canaanite mother whose daughter was tormented by a demon is troubling at best. I want to recast this interaction, using questions, which may very well have been the way Jesus interacted with this woman. The questions tell a different story:

> Just then a Canaanite woman from Tyre and Sidon, where Jesus had traveled, came out to him and started shouting, "Have mercy on me, Rabbi, Son of David; my daughter is tormented by a demon." But Jesus did not answer her plea. And his disciples urged him, saying, "Send her away, for she keeps shouting at us!" And so Jesus turned to the foreign woman and asked her, "Have you not heard me say that my mission is to the lost sheep of the house of Israel?" But the woman persisted, and knelt before him, pleading, "Lord, help her." He asked her, "Is it fair to take food intended for the children and throw it to the dogs?" And she said, "Perhaps not, yet do not even dogs eat the crumbs that fall from their master's table?" Then Jesus answered her, "Woman, great is your faith! Let it be done for you as you wish." And her daughter was healed instantly. (Matt 15:21-28, author's paraphrase)

The questions in this passage make Jesus' interaction with the woman more playful. It is hard to imagine this interaction if not playful, because otherwise Jesus is depicted as judgmental and narrow-minded. Even if playful, however, this strange little story is about a woman who with her question pushes Jesus to see a more inclusive mission. His mission is not to Jews alone, but to all of God's children, even this woman's tormented daughter. In all four Gospels, Jesus is depicted as enjoying questions from others and offered to others.

A teacher who asks lots of questions and does not need to provide immediate answers to the student is one who loves questions. Jesus shaped a questioning community, where his closest disciples felt very comfortable asking him questions and receiving his questions.

From the four Gospels, one gets the sense that people around Jesus were always trying to get him to state more plainly who he was and the nature of his mission. Typically, he would side-step such attempts at easy answers. It is impossible to reduce Jesus' life to a cliché, a formula, a tightly-reasoned argument, or a creed.

No Easy Answers

What a gift the church could offer seekers if it cherished questions! What a message: "In this community, we will not ridicule your questions; we will not condemn or disallow your questions; we will not rush your questions; and we will not diminish your questions by attempting to answer them for you."

This is not to say that someone's spiritual laws, or another's steps to salvation, or another's creed are wrong. They likely are an authentic response to one person's questions of faith. And they may, as testimonials, offer something of value to other seekers and their questions. But one person's "answers" never completely speak to another person's "questions."

A good teacher is not someone who thrusts information upon students. In this technological age, information is literally at one's fingertips, without the need for a teacher. A good teacher now, as in Jesus' day, is someone who helps students develop a passion for worthy questions.

When I entered Mr. Ward's classroom in the ninth grade, I was scared to death. I had heard he was the toughest teacher in the high school. I also had heard that he was the most beloved teacher. In four years, Jim Ward taught me to respect and honor my questions; few others have ever given me such a gift.

The truth of it is, I cannot answer your questions. Neither can any preacher or theologian. You are free to settle for my answers, but you are the only person who can adequately answer your questions. You are the only person who can follow your questions' leading, who can live with your questions and cherish your questions.

There have been regrettable instances when I have been so enamored by my answers to someone else's struggles that I have pushed them too hard, and in so doing have robbed those people of their ability to struggle with their own questions. I have no right to squelch someone's questions and interrupt their lead.

The core of the word question is "quest." Questions can set us off on a quest. Many people will not budge until their questions are answered. But if God is in some of our questions, we will do well to engage in a quest for the answers and consider the path of our walk as holy ground. The quest may very well be as important as the answer or response that comes to us as a result of the quest.

At issue here is not informational questions. At issue with most of Jesus' questions were not the questions people had, but the questions that had them. There are questions of our own making. But there are also questions that come from beyond ourselves, that follow us throughout our lives. Such questions can be frightening, paralyzing, or consuming. And yet, it does little good to run from such questions, because questions have a way of pursuing us and reemerging later.

If God is in the central questions of our lives, the core questions, the soul questions, then by cherishing the questions, we also cherish God. If God gives us certain questions, then we should cherish those questions as gifts from God. A hurried or cursory attempt to answer those questions diminishes the richness of God's gift.

Jesus practiced the belief that questions are important to the spiritual life. It was one key to the vitality of his faith. Persons who do not ask questions, and churches that do not encourage questions, will tend to have a stagnant spiritual life. God is not only in the answers, but in the questions. Questions worth following are those that point beyond themselves, helping us appreciate mystery and wonder. Rainer Maria Rilke, in *Letters to a Young Poet,* offers this truth:

> You are so young, so much before all beginning, and I would like to beg you, dear Sir, as well as I can, to have patience with everything unresolved in your heart and to try to love the questions themselves as if they were locked rooms or books written in a very foreign language. Don't search for the answers, which could not be given to you now, because you would not be able to live them. And the point is, to live everything. Live the questions now. Perhaps then, someday far in the future, you will gradually, without even noticing it, live your way into the answer.[2]

There is such a thing, however, as fear of answers or reticence to move from questions to answers. Questions involve a quest to be followed, not static words to be savored. There comes a time to declare ourselves, to cling to the truth, to affirm all that can be affirmed, and to allow our lives to be graced by wisdom. Jesus certainly used a questioning style in his teaching, but it was also his occasional willingness to step beyond questions and declare himself that appeared so unusual to his hearers, leading them to say, "This rabbi speaks with authority."

Conclusion

Questions are valid because they lead us somewhere. Their quest leads us to answers, to clues, to responses, to truth. The spirit of truth leads us on our quest to the truth. Jesus once taught, "If you continue in my word, you are truly my disciples; and you will know the truth, and the truth will make you free" (John 8:31b-32).

Paint Jesus as the Lover of Questions. And as the Living Rabbi today, envision what question Jesus might be asking of you.

Notes

[1] Marie Livingston Roy, *Alive Now,* March/April 1981 (Nashville: The Upper Room) 3.

[2] Rainer Maria Rilke, *Letters to a Young Poet* (Boston: Shambhala Pocket Classics, 1993) 49-50.

Chapter 6
Jesus as Risen Rabbi
John 20:16

Beginning with the book of Romans, most of the remainder of the New Testament is actual correspondence of early church leaders. Some of the Letters were written by the apostle Paul and named for the earliest Christian churches he founded and to whom he later wrote. These letters are the earliest writings found in the New Testament, written beginning a little more than fifteen years after Paul became a follower of Christ. The first letter, 1 Thessalonians, was written about 50 A.D., a mere two decades after Jesus' crucifixion.

If you scan page after page of these earliest Christian writings, you will discover something startling. They contain almost no mention of Jesus' birth, life, teachings, healings, and ministry. They seemingly begin with Jesus' death on the cross and his resurrection. Later writings, the four Gospels, placed at the beginning of the New Testament, relate the stories about Jesus' life and ministry. Why this arrangement?

Two Congregations

Just after Jesus' death, his discipling community migrated from Galilee to Jerusalem, a cosmopolitan center in the Roman Empire. Different language groups coexisted in the city. Its urban environment offered more "space" for the early believers to practice their faith. Those who knew Jesus firsthand spoke Aramaic, the common language of Palestinian Jews and the language Jesus himself spoke. Everything they remembered about Jesus, as well as all of his proverbs, parables, and teachings, was in Aramaic.

But the first discipling community in Jerusalem was broadening. Soon there were added Greek-speaking followers (Acts 6:1). We have reason to believe that the seven new apostles who were appointed by the original disciples (v. 5) were given leadership over the Greek-speaking congregation (vv. 1-6). This new congregation was composed largely of later converts, likely not persons who knew Jesus firsthand. Relations between the two groups resulted in some tensions. And it was the Greek-speaking group that largely ran into persecution from other Jews. Stephen was a leader of this newer group, and his stoning and death prompted a hasty departure by the Greek-speaking Christians from Jerusalem. Martin Hengel explained subsequent events.

> An understandable consequence of the martyrdom of Stephen was the persecution and expulsion of the Jewish-Christian "Hellenists" from the Holy City (Acts 8:1, 4; 11:19). . . . Possibly this sudden expulsion from Jerusalem . . . was a first stimulus to direct their mission towards the despised in Palestine, the "marginal settlers" of Israel, the heretical Samaritans and the pagan godfearers. . . . At the time when Paul was called, which cannot have been very long after the murder of Stephen, the mission to the Gentiles apart from the law was evidently still completely new. It was carried on a short time later in a really systematic way and on a large scale only by the community in the great city of Antioch (Acts 11:19ff.). . . . On the other hand, the violent "purge" within the Hellenistic synagogue communities in Jerusalem may have had only a marginal effect on the Aramaic-speaking majority of the population of Jerusalem. The local Jewish Christians were only indirectly affected by the catastrophe which descended upon the sister community of the Hellenists.[1]

The original eyewitnesses to Jesus' ministry were mostly left behind in Jerusalem (Acts 8:1). The two congregations, speaking different languages, one largely eyewitnesses to Jesus' ministry and the other not, had only a brief time together, and then were separated by external, oppressive forces. The two congregations remained in relationship, but geography alone created isolation.

In the ensuing years, Paul joined the Greek-speaking congregation. This group, faithful to their understanding and experience of what it meant to live "in Christ," became an expansive and exciting group, developing a christology, a missiology, and an ecclesiology. Because they did not have immediate access to Jesus' teachings, his own remembered words and stories about his healings and interactions during his ministry years, they built their faith upon what they did have access to: knowledge of his death and resurrection and firsthand experience of his crucified and resurrected presence in their community.

A Jewish rabbi, now deceased, made less sense to those early Greek-speaking Christians. They might admire such a martyr and attempt to commit his teachings to memory, but this could not contain

Jesus as Risen Rabbi

the explosive nature of their faith. They did not follow a dead rabbi, but the Living Lord! They did not think of Jesus as teacher but as Lord and Savior. The title lord very likely went through a subtle transformation from being an honorary title for a rabbi to expressing the lordship of Jesus Christ over all of life.

Pauline theology made no place for Jesus as rabbi. And so the expansive and creative Greek-speaking side of the early church had lost the sense of Jesus as a teacher in the present tense. They likely knew that he was once known as a rabbi, but that had little relevance to his post-resurrection life.

The older church, the so-called mother church in Jerusalem, conserved the words of Jesus. In the Jerusalem church, in Aramaic, the oral tradition of Jesus was kept alive. Whether the gospel should be spread to non-Jews remained suspect among those folk (Acts 15:1-2). While the Greek-speaking church was taking the gospel to the Gentile world, the Jerusalem church was committing Jesus' ministry and teachings to heart. Jesus the Rabbi had to have been known to them.

During this time, on the Greek-speaking side, Paul's ministry occurred, and that is likely why Paul's letters focus upon Jesus' death and resurrection and ignore his ministry as a rabbi. Paula Fredriksen notes,

> About Jesus of Nazareth Paul evinces little interest. He reports few of (Jesus') sayings and admits freely that he had not known Jesus "according to the flesh." Paul sees Jesus' significance and status as eschatological redeemer granted not in his biography (where he was born, what he preached, whom he called) but in his resurrection . . . Paul's gospel, accordingly, relates not Jesus' teachings, but Paul's teachings about the meaning of Christ's resurrection. . . . Finally, Paul derives his authority as apostle not from any contact with the historical Jesus but from his experience of the Risen Christ (Gal 1:12-16; 1 Cor 9:1).[2]

Then something happened. Because of a Jewish political revolt, the Roman army entered Jerusalem, and by C.E. 70 had completely destroyed the city and drove off all of its inhabitants as punishment for their disloyalty to Caesar. The Jerusalem church had to relocate along with all the other inhabitants of the city.

Where did they flee? To their spiritual cousins, of course, in the Greek-speaking churches of Asia Minor. And they took with them, to

Corinth, to Thessalonica, to Ephesus, to Antioch, stories about Rabbi Jesus, stories that some of the newer Gentile and Jewish converts may never have heard.

A new kind of literature emerged in the dynamic mixing of these two communities. The four Gospels tell the stories of Jesus' life, teachings, and ministry, while reflecting the early Gentile church's experience of Jesus as Lord and Savior.

Many have thought the Gospels to be a stroke of inspired genius, bringing together the remembered oral tradition from the Jerusalem church and the explosively creative theology of the Greek-speaking churches. A new literary device was created, a storytelling, truth-sharing gospel.

Yet the church today has never quite overcome Paul's hesitancy in speaking of Jesus as rabbi. How can the church follow a dead rabbi? Mary Magdalene points the way.

A Woman's Testimony

Mary Magdalene went to the tomb early on the first day of the week after Jesus was buried. She noticed that the stone had been rolled away. She ran to Simon Peter and others with the disturbing news that Jesus' body had been removed from the tomb. They ran and saw what Mary had told them, and then "returned to their homes" (John 20:10b).

"But Mary stood weeping outside the tomb. As she wept, she bent over to look into the tomb." She saw a man standing beside her whom she supposed to be the gardener. The man said to her, "Woman, why are you weeping? Whom are you looking for?" She answered him through her tears, "Sir, if you have carried him away, tell me where you have laid him, and I will take him away." And the man said to her, "Mary!" (vv. 11, 15).

Mary turned toward him again and said in Aramaic, "Rabbouni!" Jesus told her not to cling to him but to go to the disciples and tell them what she had witnessed. "Mary Magdalene went and announced to the disciples, 'I have seen the Lord'; and she told them that he had said these things to her" (v. 18).

Mary was the first follower to see the Risen Lord. She called him "Rabbouni"—Rabbi, Teacher. The church has never quite found Mary believable. Indeed, in the Gospel of Luke, it was a group of women, including Mary Magdalene, who had come to the tomb to anoint his body with burial spices. The women ran to the disciples to share the news, but their words "seemed to them an idle tale, and they did not believe them" (Luke 24:11). The women's testimony was minimized as "women's chatter." Once again, women had lost their objectivity; they had lost their hold on the truth. They had been crying instead of thinking. Mark also reports that "Jesus appeared first to Mary Magdalene," but "when they heard that he was alive and had been seen by her, they would not believe it" (16:11).

Women have so often been discredited as valid witnesses, their words and their emotions held suspect. The Risen Lord appeared first to the women. The four Gospels agree on this fact. Yet the other disciples would not believe their testimony.

The church still does not believe Mary or hear her word; it overlooks her testimony. All through Mary's days with Jesus, she had called him Rabbi. Throughout this time, she cherished him for the intimate times they had shared; she called him by the affectionate term Rabbouni! She first knew him as a risen rabbi.

Why, then, has the church never followed Mary's leading? Why have we failed to call him our risen rabbi? Why have we failed to see him not only as a teacher "back then," but with Mary also see him as a teacher now, a resurrected teacher, a risen rabbi? Why do we still refuse to take a woman's word for it?

The Post-Resurrection Rabbi

If you study the resurrection appearances of Jesus more closely, you may be amazed to discover that Jesus' role as teacher did not end with his death. In all four Gospels, the resurrected Jesus continues with the disciples primarily as a teacher. Jesus' only appearance in Matthew to the eleven disciples includes his command to them to teach others "to obey everything that I have commanded you" (28:19-20).

When a resurrected Jesus appeared with two disciples on the road to Emmaus, he interpreted to them the things about himself in the scriptures (Mark 16; Luke 24). Later the two disciples remembered how their hearts were burning within while the Risen Rabbi was "opening the scriptures" to them (Luke 24:32).

The resurrected Jesus appeared before the disciples and "upbraided them for their lack of faith and stubbornness" because they wouldn't believe Mary and the other first witnesses (Mark 16:14). We see a typical rabbi's interaction with his disciples. Also, the resurrected Jesus had breakfast with several disciples. The famous teaching incident with Peter followed, with Jesus using a rabbinical technique of repeating a question, "Do you love me?" (John 21).

In other words, seven of the twelve reported instances of Jesus' resurrection interactions had to do with his teaching ministry or acting as a rabbi with the disciples. Clearly, the Gospel writers did not conclude Jesus' teaching activity with his death. After his death, the resurrected Lord acted as the Risen Rabbi. How seldom we recognize this. Why for the church has this been such a secondary role?

Jesus is to be our teacher, our rabbi—then, now, and always. The cross and his death were not intended to be an end to his role as our teacher. If ours is an incarnational faith, the Word made flesh, if we are to be an Easter people, we cannot leave Jesus on the cross or in the tomb. But how do we bring Jesus into the twentieth century, not just his ideas, but Jesus? How do we take that leap of faith, making Jesus believable today?

During his ministry, Jesus had a robust, definitive role as a wandering, charismatic rabbi or teacher. He died and suddenly became a nebulous, spiritualized entity. And in that transition, many of us become lost. We need a teacher today, a rabbi. If we stay with Jesus as risen rabbi, some of us may resolve our incarnational dilemma.

To think of God, to approach God, as the Creator, Son, or Holy Spirit, you have to use your imagination. You must depend upon images. You cannot just pray to "God"; something must come to mind as you pray to God. It may no longer be a grandfather with a long beard sitting on a throne in the clouds. It may not be a person or an object. But even to think of God as creative power, as transcendent mystery, as gift-giver—all these require imagination to bring to mind the one with whom you are praying.

The same is true for Jesus. Jesus as God's Son is one image, one way of relating to Jesus today. But that image is often nebulous and ties Jesus to his being a male, which is his least provocative role. He was known as teacher, called Rabbi by all who knew him. If we bring Jesus into our lives and thoughts as our rabbi or teacher, the focus is no longer upon his being a man. The focus is upon what the Rabbi wants to do with us, where the Rabbi wants to be with us, and where the Rabbi stands in relation to us.

A Personal Testimony

It was the week following the trial of Rodney King, the young African-American man in Los Angeles who was mercilessly beaten by police officers while someone nearby videotaped the incident. The city was consumed with a city-wide revolt. An African-American leader in my church had been invited along with me to attend a live radio forum sponsored by a black-owned station in Philadelphia. The forum was in response to the Los Angeles revolt.

We walked into the vast auditorium where hundreds of African-Americans had gathered. It was an open microphone time on the radio. I do not think that those who planned the forum had any idea how angry the crowd was going to be.

While emotions ran high, there was nothing unruly about the crowd. But at the conclusion of the evening, I left wondering how Philadelphia had avoided a revolt in our streets. As I sat there for two hours and listened to the pain and anger of speaker after speaker, what before had seemed somewhat distant suddenly seemed real and disturbing. Grandmothers spoke with rage; deacons spoke with rage; street-wise young men spoke with rage; Muslims spoke with rage; a wealthy manufacturer spoke with rage; schoolteachers spoke with rage. The rage awakened me ever so much to the damage that the racism within me and within our dominant culture has done.

The following week I began to feel the Teacher working on me. In a midweek prayer and imaging group, I had been trying to open myself spiritually to the Resurrected Teacher. The Risen Rabbi had work to do with and on me, just as any teacher approaches the challenge of educating her students.

I knew I had been privileged during the forum to have my eyes opened, and the Teacher seemingly wanted to make sure that I saw and heard it all! I was being led to realize that I could not sit back while my African-American neighbors were in such severe pain and rage. I felt the need to recommit myself, as never before, to the undoing of racism. With others in my congregation who shared this urgency, I knew I must follow the leadership of the Risen Rabbi, just as the first disciples followed their rabbi on a liberating pilgrimage, and drop my nets and preoccupations, and follow in directions and risks I had not yet considered.

I am convinced the Risen Rabbi was working within me and on me, bringing insight and clarity, bringing meaning and resolution, bringing questions and issues to the fore, and helping me see what I must do.

Conclusion

That is how the Risen Rabbi can be our connection with the original Rabbi, still teaching, still calling, still journeying, still a part of the learning and becoming of all who are in the ongoing discipling community. The Risen Rabbi is a permanently tenured position!

Will we take a woman's word for it? No longer in human flesh, the one she had taken to be the gardener spoke her name, "Mary." She turned, and recognizing her teacher, she said, "Rabbouni!" Mary holds out that same possibility for us today. Will we turn and see our teacher, the Risen Rabbi? Or will we reduce Mary's testimony to an idle tale?

Notes

[1] Martin Hengel, *Between Jesus and Paul* (Philadelphia: Fortress Press, 1983) 24-25.

[2] Paula Fredriksen, *From Jesus to Christ* (New Haven CT: Yale University Press, 1988) 174.

Chapter 7
The Teacher Is Here and Is Calling You
John 11; Isaiah 30:19-20

Jesus loved this home in Bethany. There was no other family with whom he seemed to have been more intimate, including his own. This family argued in front of him, openly challenged him, and honored him. It surely was an unusual family in a marriage-dominated society, because from what we can ascertain, there were three unmarried siblings living together—Martha, Mary, and Lazarus. This home in this poor village was his "safe haven" whenever Jesus was in Jerusalem, less than two miles away.

All three siblings had a special relationship with Jesus. When Lazarus fell ill, the sisters sent this message to Jesus, "Lord, he whom you love is ill" (John 11:3b). The story goes on to say that Jesus "loved Martha and her sister and Lazarus" (v. 5). For a loss in this family, Jesus cried and became "greatly disturbed in spirit and deeply moved" (v. 33c). The others nearby said, "See how he loved him" (v. 36b).

By the time Jesus arrived in Bethany after having tarried for two days longer in the place where he was teaching, Lazarus had been dead for four days. Apparently the village was crowded with those who had come from the capital city to grieve with the two sisters over their brother's death. The loss of a man in a family was indeed serious, for there was a long-standing social custom of women being under the care of a man. Indeed, a widow was customarily passed from the care of a deceased brother to a living brother. Mary and Martha were not as legitimate in the public eye without Lazarus. There was much to grieve.

Martha heard that Jesus was on his way, and she went out from the village to meet him. She said to him, "Lord, if you had been here, my brother would not have died" (v. 21). It was not exactly a cordial greeting! Jesus reminded her, "Your brother will rise again" (v. 23). But Martha, influenced as she was by the teaching of the Pharisees, presumed that Jesus was referring to a resurrection of the dead at the end of the age. So Martha said, "I know that he will rise again on the last day" (v. 24).

But, ever the Teacher, especially in the midst of the laboratory of life, with grief on their hands and issues between them, Jesus began to teach Martha saying, "I am the resurrection and the life. Those who believe in me, even though they die, will live, and everyone who lives and believes in me will never die. Do you believe this?" (vv. 25-26). Martha said to him, "Yes, Lord, I believe that you are the Messiah, the Son of God, the one coming into the world" (v. 27).

Martha acknowledged that she knew who Jesus was. In this, she was one of his few followers who truly "knew who he was." The conversation continued a bit longer, and at the end of it, Jesus sent Martha on a special mission. Martha went back to the village and into their home. There her sister, Mary, was grieving along with consoling friends. The two sisters were grieving in different ways and places, characteristic of their very different personalities. Martha, ever in the hosting role, was receiving the crowds as they arrived. Mary, the more contemplative, was withdrawn inside the house, needing to process her grief out of public view. Martha entered the house and whispered to Mary in private, "The Teacher is here and is calling for you."

The Calling of a Name

Recently I was reading the book of Isaiah and was startled to encounter this unfamiliar passage where the prophet refers to God as "your Teacher," as in no other place in the Old Testament.

> Truly, O people in Zion, inhabitants of Jerusalem, you shall weep no more. He will surely be gracious to you at the sound of your cry; when he hears it, he will answer you. Though the Lord may give you the bread of adversity and the water of affliction, yet your Teacher will not hide himself any more, but your eyes shall see your Teacher. (30:19-20)

The concept of rabbi or teacher really did not emerge or have a cultural meaning for the Jews until after the pages of the Old Testament had been written. The rabbinical period began within two hundred years prior to Jesus' birth. For centuries, the ancient Jews had been reluctant for anyone to take on the title of rabbi or teacher, just as with the earlier reluctance to call any human being king. Yet, for all the occasions when Israel was "instructed" by Yahweh, the title of God as teacher occurs only this one time in the Old Testament.

The teacher of whom Isaiah prophesied was the teacher who arrived in the village of Bethany and called for Mary. The Teacher had come. He knew Mary's name and was calling for her. There is something very powerful about hearing your name called out or being asked for by name. Mary got up quickly and went to her teacher.

Once in a prayer and imaging session, I was inviting the participants to use their imaginations to hear the Teacher call their names. Some of those present blocked at that point and could not hear their name called, because somehow they knew in the calling of their name they would hear more than they were ready to hear. One person said, "I heard a name, not my actual name, but an unspoken name that captures who I am, what I'm striving to be, a name that acknowledges my journey."

Have you noticed that you never feel fully welcome in a place until someone calls you by name? Surely you have experienced the joy of hearing your name remembered and called by someone who has just met you. I am sure you remember also how much it hurt in elementary school when your detractors or friends finally found a way to make fun of your name.

Yes, I have a Social Security number. I have it memorized. I have a driver's license number, and every credit card in my wallet has my own personalized number. But those numbers are dehumanizing. The humanizing labels are our names. And on those occasions when it was said, "She spoke my name," we know that something more was meant than just the verbal pronouncement of a name. It was a recognition, a valuing, an affirmation, a cherishing, an understanding. One definition of community, as the "Cheers" TV theme song goes, is a place where "everybody knows your name."

For years I have heard of "Dr. Middleton" from my wife and her mother. He was the courageous pastor who challenged their reluctant inner city congregation to open its doors to all races. He was an expressive and prophetic preacher, a visionary leader who helped the church make decisions that to this day allow it to survive and flourish. One day Dr. Middleton asked my wife's mother to help transport black inner city children out to a suburban building for a church meeting. Apparently, it was at a time when not many members would volunteer to do this. In fact, my wife was embarrassed at transporting black children. Yet today she is proud of her mother's risk-taking commitment to a broader gospel and looks back at Dr. Middleton as a revered person in her life. It is probably one of the healthiest things in our marriage that for her, the model of being a pastor is not me but Dr. Middleton.

Dr. Middleton is now retired and serving an interim pastorate nearby. Not long ago my wife asked me to call him and set up a meeting. Before I picked up the phone, about to address this man whom I had only met once or twice, I asked her, "What do I call him?" I had only heard him referred to as "Dr. Middleton," but it sounded a bit strange to call a colleague in such a formal way.

Well, I made the call. I said, "Hello, Dr. Middleton," and told him who I was. He instantly recognized me and said, "Steve, please call me Bob." And so this hero of my wife's childhood church was suddenly "Bob." Something changed all over my wife's face, sitting next to me as I whispered, "He wants me to call him Bob." It was like a childhood hero saying, "You are now an adult; you are now on my level; we are equals." Not bad for a day's work. As we traveled down to meet them, we already had a cherished feeling.

The calling of a name . . . I think the Samaritan woman at the well said it best when, after meeting Jesus and then describing him to her friends, she said, "He told me everything I had ever done" (John 4:39). He knew everything about me; he spoke my name.

Teachable Moments

"The Teacher is here and is calling for you." What if that were true for you? What if there was a knock at your front door, and a member of your family came into your room and whispered in your ear, "The Teacher is here and is calling for you."

It is the message of the gospel, the "good news" that the Teacher is here and is calling you by name. And in the midst of this laboratory of life, in this in-between place in your life, in-between emotions, in-between decisions, in-between relationships, in-between transitions, this can be a teachable moment.

When you have a beloved brother to bury, when you have anger or resentment that someone who should have responded did not, when you have a crowd around you demanding your attention, when you have grief to work through—in the midst of it, the Teacher comes to teach. Just as a first-century rabbi had an intimate knowledge of his disciples, the Living Teacher calls you by name. The Teacher already understands you, already senses your issues, your transitions, your ambivalence, your unanswered questions. The Teacher knows where and why you stand in need of an unexpected miracle.

I have read this passage about Bethany countless times, but I have never really *heard* it. As I was instructing some seminary students in a reflection around this text, I heard one of them read this line, "The Teacher is here and is calling for you." Something in the way she read that verse struck home as if I had never heard the passage before. I realized that Mary is not the only person in history for whom this statement is true. Like Mary, the Teacher is here as well, and is calling for me.

I do not think it was coincidence that these two passages, one from Isaiah and the other from John, confronted me. Isaiah prophesied, when you see the Teacher with your own eyes, then, "when you turn to the right or when you turn to the left, your ears shall hear a word behind you, saying, 'This is the way; walk in it' " (Isa 30:21). The "word behind me" linked together the Teacher of Isaiah 30 and the Teacher who arrived in Bethany and the Teacher who arrives yet today.

Conclusion

The church's teaching and learning will be forever different if we recognize that life's teachable moments can come anytime and anywhere we are ready to encounter the Teacher. Often, we will have to find a way to get around "our agenda," as did Martha and Mary, in order to be interrupted by a Teacher whose classroom knows no bounds.

The church's teacher is the one who summons. The summons is in part the way Rabbi Jesus teaches. We see this in the way Jesus called the original disciples and in the way their long-established patterns and careers gave way to an entirely new sense of vocation. The Rabbi calls our name and, in speaking our name, issues a direction for us to follow.

The church has been very comfortable with the idea of Jesus calling us to purpose, vocation, and life's direction. When we can see that calling from a teacher, the summons itself becomes a teachable moment. We would like to respond to the summons "just as we are," and remain so, but the summons itself is transformational. In following the Rabbi, we will discover, as did his followers of old, that reality and vision will never again be the same. May Martha be our messenger as well, whispering to us the message, "The Teacher is here and is calling for you."

Chapter 8
They Had Been with Jesus
Acts 4:13

Peter and John had just healed the lame beggar on their way into the temple. The crowds were amazed. The elders and teachers of the Law had them put in jail for the night because of their teaching and likely the public stir the healing caused. They asked, "By what power and in whose name have you done this?" (Acts 4:7c). Peter "was filled with the Holy Spirit" (v. 8a) and began teaching the nation's leaders and elders. He quoted Old Testament scripture and imagery. His argument was articulate, bold, and provocative. "The officials were amazed to see how brave Peter and John were" (v. 13a).

Yet, the officials assumed these two apostles were only ordinary men and not well-educated. They were recognized as followers of Rabbi Jesus, and because Rabbi Jesus was not a respected master teacher, his disciples were not thought to be well-educated. This implies a negative judgment against Jesus as an authoritative rabbi. He likely was known as a rabbi with less-than-respectable disciples.

But the elders of the nation also knew Jesus' discipling community and were able to recognize the Rabbi in his disciples. "The officials were certain that these men had been with Jesus" (v. 13c) because of the boldness of their witness, the graciousness of their hospitality toward an "unclean man" (John 9:3, 34), their persuasive argument, their provocative use of Holy Scripture, the unorthodox wisdom of their argument, the power of their healing, and the trouble they caused for those in positions of authority. Such are the traits of those who have been with Rabbi Jesus. Are you and I as recognizable by the time we have spent with the Teacher?

The Living Teacher has a profound influence on our lives as followers. There will be moments when, like Peter and John, others will see our bold witness, our provocative insight, our healing intervention, our risking action, our controversial response, and say of us, "We are certain that you have been with Rabbi Jesus." They will know by the way we stop at the gate and "make strong" those who cannot make their own way or are excluded because of social assumptions as to their unworthiness. If we have been with Jesus, we will want others also to have that life-changing experience.

Theological Work in Meeting Rabbi Jesus

If we are to fully encounter Jesus as a living teacher, much theological work confronts us: evangelical work, christological work, biblical work, and spiritual work.

Evangelical Work

How to make Jesus accessible to each generation is the task of evangelism. Many people outside the church simply cannot relate to Christ as some ephemeral, other-worldly figure. Nor can people relate to him as a dead messianic figure from the ancient world, memorialized in stained glass windows. Jesus as living teacher is a tangible, understandable, and appealing introduction. Almost everyone has experienced great teachers to whom we are deeply indebted. It is far more difficult to have such immediate experiences of a Savior, a Lord, a miracle worker, a healer, or a "Son of man." Thinking of Jesus as a teacher can help many people form tangible connections with him. Evangelism is the work of forming connections between Christ and people's everyday experiences.

Christological Work

Who is the Second Person of the Trinity? God is the creator of the universe and source of love. The Spirit, the Third Person, is God's empowering presence among us. But who is the Second Person? Could the Second Person be the Incarnational Teacher, the one who points us toward God, who represents us to God and God to us? Jesus cannot be just an informational source about God. He cannot be just an ancient teacher who tells parables and beatitudes. Jesus mediates the transforming power of God in our lives. If Jesus is the Living Teacher, when we meet him, we discover our avenue to God. Can people today more fully understand Jesus by seeing him as their ever-present teacher?

Biblical Work

Scholars will continue to form deeper understandings of Jesus as teacher in the first century and of the Jewish/Palestinian social context of his teaching ministry and discipling community, but much of the biblical work is already there for us. We must read the most recent translations of the Gospels with an attentive eye to Jesus as teacher. We must also read the Gospels with an imaginative eye to see ourselves in Jesus' story. The Bible as the accepted authority for Christians keeps us on track and holds accountable the paradigm of Jesus as a living teacher today with its stories and accounts of Jesus as a first-century Jewish rabbi.

Spiritual Work

What is the spiritual work we must do? Is it not the relational work of cultivating connections to the Living Christ? Spiritual work prepares us to meet God in Jesus Christ. It calls for a convergence of education and spirituality in the church.

A Spirituality of Education

For many educators, even those in the church, it seems a contradiction or compromise to approach education and spirituality together. Secular education, including most Christian education, has as its aim taking into grasp that which we have not understood. Spirituality has to do with being grasped by the one beyond us. Spirituality and education seem at counter-purposes. Now the church needs to reclaim the uniqueness of Christian education as a way of bringing spirituality and education together.

One educator who speaks of a "spirituality of education" is Parker Palmer. In his book, *To Know as We Are Known: A Spirituality of Education,* he wrote,

> Prayer and analysis do not end up at the same point; where analysis aims at breaking the world into its elements, prayer aims at seeing beyond the elements into their underlying relatedness.[1]

Palmer argues against an objectifying of truth in which the subject is divorced from the "object" to be learned.

> Where conventional education deals with abstract and impersonal facts and theories, an education shaped by Christian spirituality draws us toward incarnate and personal truth. In this education we come to know the world not simply as an objectified system of

empirical objects in logical connection with each other, but as an organic body of personal relations and responses, a living and evolving community of creativity and compassion.[2]

In Christian education today, we do not lack trained educators, quality educational resource materials, or concern, or effort. Too often what is missing is the church's teacher. Those who would direct learning in the church need to enable people to encounter and learn from the Teacher.

As facilitators of learning, we introduce persons to the Rabbi. Beyond meeting the Rabbi in the Gospels, we can also introduce persons to the Living Rabbi through these disciplines: silence and meditation, prayer, communal discernment, intuition and imagination, accountability and boundaries, surprise and interruption, solitude and community.

Silence and Meditation

Silence is God's language. Throughout the pages of Scripture, God speaks through silence. "Be still, and know that I am God" (Ps 46:10a). When we can say, "For God alone, my soul waits in silence" (62:1a), we are ready to hear God.

We enter silence not for a desired outcome, but for the experience of encountering God. With silence, I do not mean the absence of noise. Silence here is a meditative term for quiet centering, soulful focusing upon encounter with God.

My encounter can be with the second person of God, the Living Teacher, whom I meet in silence. I can meet Rabbi Jesus by quiet meditation upon a Gospel story in which he offered himself to someone, just as today he offers himself to me. Jesus was constantly pulling aside some of his disciples to a remote hillside for silent prayer. I can learn from the Living Teacher by many forms of meditative centering. In so doing, I experience the spirituality of education.

Prayer

We can speak with the Living Teacher, opening our thoughts, yearnings, hopes, and cares. Our prayers too often are dominated by requests or direction. We might do well to pray to Rabbi Jesus with questions rather than requests.

Rabbis typically used questions as a primary teaching style. Transforming interaction with the Living Rabbi may come through "prayerful questioning." At the start of the day for the past year, I have asked three questions that have made me more receptive for an encounter with the Living Rabbi:

What do you have to teach me?
How will you transform me?
Where will you lead me?

Personal questions such as these are best posed and tested in community. The prayerful questions can be made plural and asked by discipling communities:

What do you have to teach us?
How will you transform us?
Where will you lead us?

Answers to questions such as these do not often come in one moment. But as we begin to live out the questions, the Living Teacher shapes these into prayerful actions.

Communal Discernment

Discernment is an autobiographical activity. In other words, it is learning to recognize God's story in our stories. It requires the courage to see God in our lives and the discipline to refrain from doing so too presumptively. Discernment is an "inward knowing," the kind of knowing that "comes to you" from beyond your own mental manipulations. Discernment is a reflective, meditative knowing.

Communal discernment is the corrector of personal discernment. Some things seem so very obvious and true to me until I see them through the eyes of others. In the personal correspondence of the apostle Paul we occasionally see the limits of his personal discernment, for instance, when he wrote, "Does not nature itself teach you that if a man wears long hair, it is degrading to him, but if a woman has long hair, it is her glory? For her hair is given to her for a covering" (1 Cor 11:14-15). Here Paul needed someone to challenge his bias. Nature does not teach that men should wear only short hair, nor that long hair "glorifies" a woman. Paul's culture taught that. We engage in communal discernment to be able to correct such distorted assumptions. Discernment lends credibility to the spirituality of education.

Intuition and Imagination

Actually, we cannot discern without our intuition; neither can we pray without our imagination. These gifts, given in varying degrees to all, enable us to engage in a spirituality of education. Intuition involves trusting the way of inner knowing, the sensing of truth. I suppose it is the opposite of scientific or objective knowing, though no scientist will make much of a difference without deploying intuition.

Imagination is just as essential to prayer. How can we pray to God, whom we cannot see, and whose voice cannot be audibly heard? How can we "speak" to God without using our imagination? We are like the little boy who chatters for an hour with his lifeless doll. Watch him, and the doll seems anything but lifeless! If you were watching people at prayer for the first time, you would surely ask the same question, "With whom are they communicating? To whom are they speaking?" We all have images of God, even if we have grown beyond anthropomorphic pictures of God. Rabbi Jesus can be an image of God, the Living Teacher, with whom we speak in prayer.

Accountability and Boundaries

I grew up in the 1960s, with the typical aversion to accountability and boundaries. I was an advocate of free speech and free expression, and to this day I still resist having my freedom cramped or limited. As I have learned from life's experiences, however, nothing really changes unless I am held accountable, hopefully in mutual relationships. Structures of accountability are critical to the spirituality of education. I cannot be a disciple of Rabbi Jesus by myself. I must be in accountable community.

I must be in a community with boundaries also, so that healing and freedom can be experienced within those boundaries. I know from personal experience that there are simply too many opportunities to hurt and be hurt unless boundaries are clearly established within accountable Christian community. Rabbi Jesus gave amazing freedom, but he also set boundaries for the original disciples, and so must we today. Boundaries rule out destructive and evil attitudes and behaviors, and encourage hopeful and constructive ones instead.

A spirituality of education will occur within a community marked by accountability and boundaries, so that we can respond with trust to the initiatives of the Living Teacher in our midst.

Surprise and Interruption

Transformation happens to us, and rarely in our own timing. Whenever we ask God to do something "on our time line," the prayer is likely ill-advised. Rather, we should pray to understand God's timing. This involves trying to let go of control, to the extent that we are open to surprise and interruption. God's call in my life has most frequently come as an interruption to my frantic attempts to be in ministry.

Typically, nothing happens unless the interruption becomes a "teachable moment." Unless I see the hand of the Living Teacher in the holy interruption, there will be nothing holy in it for me. Often, God speaks in ways and through persons who stretch me beyond my assumptions and bias.

Solitude and Community

Usually, we encounter the Living Rabbi in solitude and community. Too often, solitude is hard to handle. I tend to be a "people-person." Thinking aloud, for example, is often as productive as thinking alone. Even so, without solitude, my life becomes overwhelmed with mechanical interactions that lack fulfillment. I can encounter Rabbi Jesus in solitude.

Christianity is not a solitary religion, however. It is meant for community. Just as the Risen Rabbi appeared to the Twelve as they had gathered, or to Peter and the other disciples while fishing in the sea, or to the two disciples on the road to Emmaus, so does the Risen Rabbi appear to the church gathered together. Intimacy and solitude are the primary contexts in which I have encountered the Teacher.

A Transformational Mandate
of Christian Education Today

The teaching and learning that come from Rabbi Jesus are not for the purpose of being "well-educated" or for impressing others with our knowledge or spirituality. Nor is it to earn a credential, because the world never has respected this rabbi's credentials. Disciples of the Teacher will forever be held suspect. Because this rabbi's wisdom is subversive, the comfortable and complacent cast a wary eye upon us.

The teaching and learning in Jesus' discipling community enable us to become open to transformation as agents of God's love for others and for the world. The transformational mandate of Christian education speaks to the time we spend with the Rabbi:

- the ways we live for our most teachable moments
- our passion for waiting upon and listening for the Rabbi's voice
- our willingness to be held accountable by the discerning voices in our faith communities and in Holy Scripture
- our risking as we follow the Rabbi's leading

Christian education calls for a prayerful posture of "sitting at the Rabbi's feet." It does not revolve around dispensing information about Christian doctrines, morals, and Bible stories. These become important to Christian education only as they undergird our time with the Rabbi. We must move our focus from informing toward transforming.

Apart from a perfunctory prayer that may be uttered at the beginning or end of a lesson, today's teachers in the church have held closely to what they know about being a Christian or studying the Bible. The paradigm must change. The church's most imaginative and spiritual moments must occur in its classrooms and discipling groups. This will seem an oddity to educators trained in secular disciplines as well as to those in the church trained to follow them.

The officials looked upon Peter and John as "not well educated," even though they had devoted years as disciples of Jesus. The church has but one teacher, and the four Gospels serve as a correcting, introducing guide in our prayerful interaction with the Teacher. Rabbi Jesus did not start a school, nor is our primary calling to acquire vast knowledge about Jesus' teachings or to commit to memory the Living Sage's proverbs. Teaching and learning as followers of Rabbi Jesus help us to better walk in his way. It was a risky pilgrimage to which he invited Andrew and Simon and the Samaritan woman at the well, and to which he invites us today. The Rabbi's path invites us to healing, and through us, the world.

In this paradigm of education as transformation, education within the church and the mission of the church become one. The transformation we so need for ourselves is the very transformation the world is awaiting.

Time with the Rabbi

To experience the transformation offered by Rabbi Jesus, and to share that transformation in the church, we must spend time with him. Consider these five suggestions.

(1) *Find the right moment.* It must be a moment that is not compressed by deadlines or distractions. It should be a regular moment, a moment you set aside intentionally. It need not be a long period.

(2) *Find a "teachable place."* Locate a trusting place in your imagination. Let it be a place where you can return again and again. It could be an actual place where you have experienced transformation in the past. It could be a place where a "teachable moment" has occurred. It could be a biblical setting that is evocative and rich in meaning for you. You could view this as a haven, retreat, or place of engagement.

(3) *Envision the Rabbi.* Use the portraits in this book, and envision the Charismatic Teacher, the Subversive Sage, the Transforming Teacher, the Lover of Questions, the Risen Rabbi. You might find it helpful to picture a first-century Jewish rabbi or some composite of the great teachers in your life. Your vision of the Rabbi might be a contemporary woman, an older person, or not a person at all. You might envision the Rabbi as a discerning presence.

(4) *Await the Rabbi's voice.* It requires intuition and discernment to hear the Rabbi's voice. Since you will not hear an audible voice, the "hearing" must be of the soul. With discipline, return again and again, quieting your soul, emptying the crowded places within. Be still and await the Teacher's voice. Like all meditative work, this requires practice and discipline. You might center upon a question, such as, "What do you have to teach me?" In reality, the voice might not come at all in the stillness. The quiet waiting might better prepare you to hear the voice through the words of another person or through another

circumstance. The waiting can be a time of emptying yourself and making yourself more receptive.

(5) *Move into a scriptural encounter with the Rabbi.* Select one encounter that Rabbi Jesus had with someone in scripture. Enter into the story as a first-person participant. Become a bystander toward whom Jesus next focused his attention, or become a friend of the person whom Jesus taught or healed. Through your imagination, allow yourself to be drawn into an encounter with the Rabbi through scripture's story.

Personal Testimony

Rabbi Jesus is a regular part of my prayer life. I don't picture his face so much as his persona, the Rabbi's ways, a captivating person, an authoritative teacher, spellbinding eyes, a very wise person, transforming and healing. Through meditation and prayer, I interact with the Living Rabbi. I can be in the Rabbi's presence. I can sense the Rabbi's leading. I can, on occasion, hear the Rabbi's "voice." I can sometimes intuit the Rabbi's subversive wisdom. And on occasion, I can look back over my experiences and observe when the Living Teacher was walking quietly nearby and know that the Teacher was alive within me in those moments. And those moments have made all the difference.

Notes

[1] Parker Palmer, *To Know as We Are Known: A Spirituality of Education* (San Francisco: Harper & Row, 1983) 19.
[2] Ibid., 14-15.

You Say a Teacher He Can Be?

You say a teacher he can be?
Well, he's not been as one to me!
He is my Lord and Savior, too!
He'll heal the wounds of me and you.

I'd think as Rabbi he'd be less
than what I need or I profess?
However wise his stories be,
will clever proverb set me free?

Not in a lecture or a class,
nor in the wisdom I amass,
could e'er contain my Jesus, he,
Christ of the living, Christ for me!

But what if he did ask me, Why
not be my Teacher and Rabbi?
What if he taught me how to live?
How to be called and how to give?

What if his stories set me free?
What if his truth was Truth for me?
What if I missed my Rabbi now?
What tragic loss would I allow?

I would be still and hear him speak!
With open mind, his truth I'll seek!
He'll touch my bias, change my greed,
This Risen Rabbi is my need.

Text: © 1995 by Stephen D. Jones
Hymn Tune: O WALY WALY, LM, #392